Stop The Saboteurs

Conquer Negative Thoughts
that Hurt Your Revenue
and Your Brand

Paula Hope

Manor House

Library and Archives Canada
Cataloguing in Publication

Hope, Paula, author
   Stop the saboteurs : conquer negative thoughts that harm your brand / Paula Hope.

ISBN 978-1-897453-96-4 (paperback).

ISBN 978-1-8974539-71-5 (bound).

   1. Success in business. 2. Business referrals. 3. Business networks. 4. Consultants. 5. Self-esteem. I. Title.

HF5386.H66 2015   650.1   C2015-904713-7

Thanks to Trevor Stooke for Cover art/design: "A representation of the negative thoughts that often cloud an entrepreneur's mind. It has elements of an ominous tempest, complete with lightning and swirling spirits, that sometimes overwhelm us and keep us from reaching our full potential. In essence, this negative mind storm between our ears is the Saboteur," – Trevor Stooke.

Full Cover design: Donovan Davie and Michael B. Davie

We gratefully acknowledge the financial support of the Government of Canada through Book Fund Canada, Dept. of Canadian Heritage.

Published August 10th, 2015, Manor House Publishing Inc. First Edition – 192 pages – All rights reserved. www.manor-house.biz (905) 648-2193

Disclaimer: All of the characters in this book are fictional. Only the emotions are very, very real, especially those of the author.

To my clients, thank you. I will always treasure the trust and confidence you have placed in me. I am also deeply grateful to the Monday Morning Referral Tip readers and to Salma Burney, whose help with technology has been invaluable.

Acknowledgements

No one is more surprised than me that I wrote this book. So I have many people to thank for this unexpected accomplishment. At the same time, I always liked the short Oscar speeches.

First things first, I would like to thank Dr. Laura Crawford for her contribution to the "Body First" theme of the book. To have her join me in the writing of my first book has been delightful. I would also like to thank her for the outstanding advice that she has given me for the proactive management of my own body, giving me the strength that I needed.

To my book coach and editor, Susan Crossman, thank you so much for your support and wisdom. You are one of the key reasons this book came to be. You will be the wind under my wings for my future books. And to my publisher, Michael Davie of Manor House Publishing Inc., I would like to express my deepest gratitude for bringing this book, and I hope many other ones, to fruition.

Thank you to Salma, my virtual assistant, who waited Sunday after Sunday for the last five years for the next week's Monday Morning Referral Tip to send out to my network. The weekly discipline of creating those tips has led to writing this book.

To Trevor, thank you for the brilliant design of my book cover. As always, you came through with the best. Thank you, Warren, for the outstanding video.

Thank you to my many clients, thank you for your business. I am especially delighted to be your new business and professional development partner.

To my first business network, the Canadian Office Products Association (COPA), and to all of my other networks, including the Oakville Chamber of Commerce, International Factoring Association –Canadian Chapter, E-Spot, Mississauga Board of Trade, BNI, Referral Institute and to the special members of my own referral marketing group, a big thank you. And finally, my gratitude to my first referral partner, Grace Attard, and to my other referral partners, Husam Jandal, Adrian Herschell, Maria da Silva and a few more who wish to be anonymous.

I would like to send out a special thank you to all of the sales professionals with whom I have worked, especially my former colleagues from Ko-Rec-Type. I learned so much from you. And speaking of KRT and Ko-Rec-Type-Europe, I am grateful to Paul Hudson in Ireland who stuck his neck out for me and I hope that he does not regret it.

To my colleagues at the Referral Institute in the US, and world-wide, I would like to thank you so much for your collegiality and support. A special thank you to Mike Macedonio, President of the Referral Institute as well as Dawn Lyons, and Eddie Esposito. And to Dr. Ivan Misner, founder of BNI and the Referral Institute, how can I thank you enough for bringing referral marketing into the limelight where it belongs? I am so grateful.

To my stepfamily, The Humes, I must seem eccentric to you at times, and I hope that you view "my writerly ways" kindly. Thank you so much for your much-appreciated acceptance.

To my mother, Muriel Hope, and my siblings, Ted Hope and Pam Hope, thank you so much for being there for me, always. To the Pinches, Hopes and Browns, I am delighted to be a member of our family, with so many rich stories and writers, with special thanks to Charles Pinch, the first family member to be a writer. To the Farquharsons, thank you for the longevity and the local legacy that has given me street cred in the Blue Mountains, with special thanks to Tom England, my first buddy.

To all of my girlfriends, I appreciate your friendship, fun and laugher so much. A special shout-out to all of my tennis friends, especially the members of our tennis and "yet to be named" book club. Now we have two writers in our midst. To the Balm Beach Babes, I am so grateful for our traditions and good times. Special thanks to Tracy Blyth and Candace Castro for their friendship and support.

To the incomparable Dr. Denise Jacques, thank you for honouring me with your lifelong friendship.

To my daughter, Liz, I hope that this book helps further to smooth your pathway to success, whatever you wish it to be.

And to, David Hume, my life partner, thank you for taking such good care of me. You make me think of the Beach Boys song, 'God only knows where I'd be without you." Certainly I would not be penning this book. Please do stick around for the next book, and the ones after that.

Finally, thank you to my father for my wonderful last name, Hope. What a gift, among many.

Contents

Preface: You Are Not Alone

In retrospect, I realize I had been bored, truly bored, with the routine of my role as an executive. My work had become soulless. I was losing my *joie de vivre*. I was "of a certain age," and my personal responsibilities had diminished somewhat. I had worked forever to support others. I was living in dangerous times for my own selfhood and it was time. Time to move on.

To move on into the life that I really wanted. Where I could do what I loved and let the money follow, find my bliss and live happily ever after. I could experience the zen of working from my own creativity and be rewarded for my courage by unimaginable wealth. I knew that having my own consulting business was what I wanted. I could do it. I had lots to offer and I was going to get out there and grab it all by the tail.

I was brimming with conviction, passion, and experience and, of course, confidence. Except I wasn't. Brimming with confidence that is. Not only was I not full of confidence, I was missing a lot of it. In fact, I had none left.

I realized that I was terrified. Terrified of *actually* living by my own wits and doing what I had always dreamed of doing.

How could this be? What the devil was getting in my way?

Overnight, I had realized the true, private hell of the professional service provider. The one that can take over your soul when you suddenly become your own brand. Everything that I said or did became the object of public scrutiny. Even more serious and debilitating was the fact that everything I said or did became the object of my *own* scrutiny. And I was bitterly unhappy with what I saw in myself.

I was forcing myself, teeming with self-doubt and sweat, to attend the same networking events that I had embraced wholeheartedly as a corporate executive. I questioned everything that I did and everything that I said. I talked too much about my business and threw out a lot of meaningless phrases. And I knew it.

I made "people" mistakes, too, that I would never have dreamt of making during my corporate life. I was burning relationships with former business clients and colleagues by over-selling and I could see that I was not clear about my message; although I had a vision of what I wanted my business to look like, I disliked myself for my lack of definition.

I *was* my brand and, with each passing day of *being* my brand, I fell deeper and deeper into my own spiral of fear, uncertainty and doubt, known as FUD in the training world.

I have never forgotten the special form of terror that I felt at the beginning of my consulting career.

I came to realize that when you are the brand, the real battle is within.

After I had moved past this initial paralyzing phase in my business, the same immobilizing panic would return every time I realized there were no new clients on the horizon. This panic became far too familiar over my years of owning a professional service business, even as the business grew and I mixed my consulting with training, coaching and speaking services.

The sickening feeling in the pit of my stomach was an experience that I thought was totally of my own making. It sounds strange now, but I felt isolated and alone every time that dread would visit me ... until I saw that same terror on the drawn faces of my fellow entrepreneurs. They talked too much, too, and muddled their way through—just like me! They were scared, too!

I discovered that I was not alone in my despair as a professional service provider. There were many others who were terrified by the responsibility of generating their own revenue. They were overwhelmed by the realization that, "If it is to be, it is up to me."

Learning more about coaching allowed me to admit to my own fears, and it became easier to recognize those fears in others as I encountered people in my own network. I began to study the emotions within myself and others with a morbid fascination. I eventually could give a name to these wretched feelings that occur when transition conspires with the sudden "you are the brand" reality—it can create a full-blown identity crisis. I named these horrible beings, these embodied fears **"The Saboteurs."**

I started to share my experiences with the dreaded Saboteurs in my weekly blogs, which I called the Monday Morning Referral Tips. I chose to publish on Mondays as I knew, all too well, that the Saboteurs routinely attacked unsuspecting business professionals on Monday mornings, as they tried to plan their week.

As I developed my Monday morning following, I stopped being surprised when seemingly confident colleagues—other professional service providers, such as lawyers, accountants, engineers, architects, business consultants and coaches—would approach me at events to tell me that I had really "put my finger on their agony" in the most recent tip.

At one event, I found myself sandwiched between an accountant and a lawyer, both of whom were pouring their hearts out to me at the same time about their own personal Saboteurs! I learned the term "rainmaker" and came to realize that reaching the partner level of a professional service firm has as much to do with the partner's ability to create new business for the firm as it does with that person's technical ability to practice professionally. "Ah," I thought, "so working at a "big name" professional service organization does not necessarily exempt you from a sales role."

I thought of all of the people who went into the professional service world to avoid sales, only to discover that they had run straight into the very fate that they had tried so hard to avoid. They had to become a brand while working in a corporation. How surprising and unsettling for them. This was definitely not what they had signed up for, after years of extra study and sacrifice to earn their accreditation.

More recently, I began to embrace my responsibility of being the public voice of the private hell of those who have the courage to be their own brand. I continued writing my weekly Monday Morning Referral Tips, helping business professionals grow their new business development acumen and warning them about the Saboteurs. In the Saboteurs' honour (or dishonour), I developed my training and coaching curricula to help business professionals grow their networking, referral-building and sales-closing skills so they would have an ongoing program to truly manage their Saboteurs.

Every year my readers receive 52 new Monday Morning Referral Tips. The subject matter of each tip varies, and I have tackled topics as diverse as "The 37 Conversations to Have with Your Referral Partner" to "The 20 Components of a Referral or High-Touch Marketing Plan." There is always much to write, speak, teach and coach about when it comes to how important it is for business professionals to build, leverage and exploit their social capital to grow a successful business or practice.

And yet, with the fresh arrival of every new client, I have been reminded of the Saboteurs. Always, always, the Saboteurs have made themselves known in so many ways within the inner landscapes of my clients. They manifest themselves quietly in the form of my clients' dislike of networking or, more powerfully, in a crippling fear of ever, ever, making sales calls by themselves. Their results tell the story.

I knew that it was time to collect all of the Saboteurs that I had learned about from my clients, and from my own rich personal experience, and expose them for the dangerous, undermining creatures that they are.

By warning you as a business professional of the Saboteurs' inevitable arrival when you become the brand, it is my goal to help you understand your real journey and prepare accordingly with coaching and training programs that will ensure your success. And, ultimately, I want to help you to embrace new business development activities joyfully.

And so, this book you're holding is for all of you business professionals who have felt immobilizing moments of fear and self-doubt when creating your own revenue. I want you to know that these paralyzing fears can and do present themselves to everyone when they become the brand. The real battle is truly within your own mind.

By exposing these Saboteurs to the light of day, by giving them names and cages, it is my plan to help you use your courage to contain them and render them impotent. Help is available and all you need to do is ask for it. The Saboteurs are wily and subversive, and their challenges can be complex; that means you need to develop all-encompassing solutions for the troubles they cause. I will be providing more on the solutions later in this book but, for now, suffice to say that there is much-needed help available to manage this internal battlefield. Business professionals need to seek out all the assistance that they can get. These are perilous waters.

For those who have the courage to live by their wits and embrace the world where "you are the brand," I want you to know that you are never alone.

Paula Hope,
Lora Bay, The Blue Mountains,
Ontario, Canada

Chapter 1:
The Private Hell of the Business Professional

I knew that we should not have met there.

The coffee shop. A public place. But he insisted. And I couldn't tell him . . . I had tried to give him as many private meeting options as I could: The Intelligent Office, where I rented space; my other office; his office.

"No," he said brightly, "this is where I meet everyone. It is a central place and works well with my schedule."

"Fine," I acquiesced. "Let's meet in your favourite place." *Let's meet in your favourite place . . . where you are going to go to your secret hell. And do in public what I know that most of us, especially men, do not want to do. Cry. Cry in public. Cry in public about your business. Or lack of it. And go to that awful, ugly place where most business professionals go when things go wrong and their revenue is scarce. To their own private, gut-wrenching hell.*

After three decades of working with business and sales professionals who are responsible for generating their own revenue, I knew the signs. This gentleman, let's call him Phil, had already shared with me that he had not signed a new customer in several months. He had to borrow money from his friends to keep going and his marriage was suffering from the impact of a serious lack of funds.

Phil was under enormous stress. He was in trouble, and he knew it. He had hit rock bottom and he did not know what to do. He had embarked upon a search for resources to assist him and, after a couple of referrals from my network, he had turned to me for help. He felt powerless to change his fate and he was lost in the tiny details of misery that attend a business that is not doing well.

In order for him to receive my assistance, I knew that Phil needed to reach down into his anguish, go to his own private hell, and decide that he did not want to be there anymore. That was my job as his prospective coach. I had to help him go to that place and see if he really wanted to make all of the changes that he was going to have to make. And, yes, cry in the process of doing his personal due diligence. Unfortunately for Phil, his tears would be in public.

As our conversation unfolded, I knew that it was going to be a long journey for Phil. The world around his business was changing rapidly. "Sand dunes in a storm" kind of changing. Phil had outgrown his particular area of expertise and his company name, logo and brand reflected that disconnect very obviously. Phil no longer had a solid business offer and, as a result, had lost his business compass some time ago. He just did not know it.

His year-long dearth of new clients most certainly reflected this unhappy state. On top of all of these challenges, Phil had avoided formal networking during his decades of owning a business. He despised the idea of having to market his services to new clients. Phil wanted to delegate new business development to someone else *now*.

And as Phil talked, he started to cry. Hard.

As is always the case, I was very touched and concerned by Phil's pain, and his tears. I looked around the coffee shop and felt grateful for the strategic choice of seating. No one could see him and he could talk freely about his thoughts and fears. And so he did.

Phil's business was in a very bad state. As he allowed his real fears to pour out of him, he admitted that he had always been lucky with new business development. He had been in the "right" business for many years and revenue had flowed to him, like water down a rock face. In the past, he had made good money, he had staff to support him and he would go out and "club the prey" for new business.

Except he really wasn't doing that. Clubbing the prey, that is. He was closing business from leads and general "word of mouth." He was not creating the environment for the prey to be clubbed, they just came running to him because his type of service had been in demand for many years.

In fact, during his 20 years of business, Phil had never done any real personal marketing. As a result, Phil had a very weak network; worse, he had not done any networking and referral-building activities in all his years of business. He hadn't given a single referral, nor helped others.

Phil was an island. Oh dear, I worried, does he have it? Will he step up?

As Phil continued with his outpouring of woe, I could see that there was much more to consider. And it wasn't good news. Phil was tired of his business and, whether or not he knew it at the time, he wanted out. He was suffering from boredom, although he could not put a name to it, yet. It was a threat to his livelihood. And to the six people at home who depended on him.

Phil's distress with his business showed in the way that he presented it. Not surprisingly, he was all over the place with his message. It took him 20 minutes to tell me what he did. And I still did not know what he did. *Not really.*

His company name and logo made no sense and they certainly did not represent his business well. The visuals were unappealing. Between Phil's long-winded message and his obscure company name and logo, it was no wonder prospective clients did not flock to him in the competitive landscape he was facing— even though he had considerable talents, and an excellent product. As the tears really started to flow, Phil got closer to the heart of the matter. To the personal side of his life, where the real roots of his hell resided. He was worried about his marriage, about disappointing his children financially and, worst of all, dealing with the resulting and constant criticism that his Mom, Dad and siblings were heaping upon him.

When we got right down to it, *Phil's business problems had nothing to do with his business.* And everything to do with the Saboteurs, negative thoughts that had set up camp in Phil's head, long ago. The real battle for Phil was, indeed, within.

Debilitating "you'll never make it" put-downs had embedded themselves in his mind. Ugly statements had grown like ivy on his internal walls and permeated his mindset until he had finally accepted the internal, insidious message they bore: he was unable to excel. The Saboteurs wanted to stop him in his tracks. And they were succeeding. No wonder Phil was in such a mess! Phil was riddled with self-doubt and he second-guessed himself constantly. His self-esteem was at rock-bottom.

As he spoke, Phil confirmed for me the fact that although he was facing many business challenges, his real problem revolved around him and his Saboteurs, not his business. He had been feeding and nurturing them for many years, decades, in fact. And how they danced in his head! He questioned everything he did.

Watch Phil's thought patterns as he lets the Saboteurs have their way with him:

> *What day is it today? Monday? I should be cold calling, knocking on doors, going to networking events, getting a new logo . . . There's no money to pay for this. . . No money coming in . . . what am I to do?. . . the kids, the kids . . . I better fix this. . . I will be disappointing my friends and family. . . again . . . like I always do. . . maybe, I'm just not good enough.*

Going down to a deeper spiral, hyperbolizing to a frenzy, as the Saboteurs giggle with glee, he would continue:

> *I'm no good . . . I should get a job . . . but where?. . . I have owned my own business all my life . . . who would want me?. . . because I am no good . . . I have nothing to offer . . . I am unemployable . . . Maybe I am just a failure . . . like everyone says . . . My family will starve . . . my wife will leave me . . . I will be homeless . . . that's what I deserve . . . I don't deserve success . . . I'm no good . . .*

All of this because there is no business?

19

Oh yes, when the Saboteurs play, they play hard. When you least need it. When you are starting out and have no revenue, when you find yourself short on new clients and at any time when you are vulnerable. That is when the Saboteurs love to play games within your head. Does that sound familiar?

Phil decided that he needed help and he wanted it now. He was going to use the last of his funds to engage my services. I thanked him, and told him that I wanted to work with him as well. Phil was a lifelong learner and I knew that this special trait would ultimately save him and his business.

I also told him that it would take at least a year to reach his goal of getting his business back to where it had been. He recognized that it had taken years to get into the position he was now in and that it would take at least a year to get out of it. And it would not stop there. He would need to maintain his new business momentum with the support of classes and coaching for as long as he owned his business. Eventually, once the Saboteurs were managed and Phil was well-trained, he would learn to enjoy new business development.

I told him that success would require intensive coaching as well as considerable new business development training in personal networking, referral-building and sales closing strategies. Fortunately, I had created the Booked Solid Program for business professionals like Phil. I showed him the diagram that I had developed to demonstrate the complexity of the task at hand.

I warned Phil that the Booked Solid program would take time and hard work, and it would involve a lot of change. But the end result would be a vast improvement over his current situation.

I also pointed out to Phil that the definition of learning is a simple two word phrase, one of the most powerful phrases in the world: "changed behaviour." The meaning is simple, but the impact is enormous.

The Booked Solid Process:

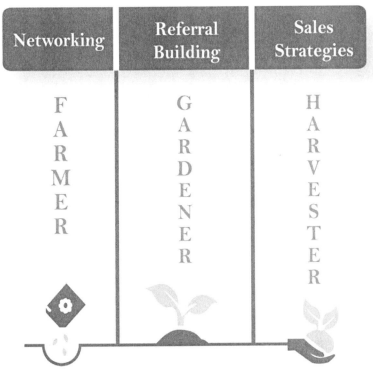

Networking	Referral Building	Sales Strategies
F A R M E R	G A R D E N E R	H A R V E S T E R

PLAN & ACCOUNTABILITY

Phil needed to be prepared for all of the changes that he would need to make in his daily routine. Creating revenue while managing his Saboteurs was an enormous undertaking. He would be required to embrace a whole new mindset about new business development and develop many new habits. Was he ready for it?

Anything, he said, anything to get out of this place. We shook hands, chatted and set a date for our first meeting. We left the coffee shop and the scene where Phil's many tears had been shed in quiet agony.

The Saboteurs had been given their notice. I did not tell Phil that he was embarking on the fight of his life.

Enter the Saboteurs:
Like many other business professionals, Phil's Saboteurs had taken over his business and personal worlds. His crippling self-doubting thoughts had rendered him helpless and vulnerable to every passing comment. He was not able to move forward without wrestling the Saboteurs at every turn. It was imperative to his business and his health that they get out of his way, and seeking help was a vital first step.

Like all business professionals who are their brand, Phil could expect to meet different Saboteurs along the way: as he expunged one Saboteur, he would meet yet another. The good news is that, like other business professionals in his shoes, Phil could expect that every Saboteur he met could be given a name, and a cage to contain it. Then, there are our very own Personal Saboteurs who visit us in the form of negative thoughts that have arisen from the wounds of childhood or other painful experiences. They can affect your business, too, if you have some unprocessed issues from the past. Tolstoy commented on dysfunctional families in *Anna Karenina* with the now-famous quip, "All happy families are alike; each unhappy family is unhappy in its own way." And so it is with the Personal Saboteurs: they plague each individual in a unique and varied fashion. If you determine that your Personal

Saboteurs are blocking your success, I suggest that you enlist the assistance of a coach, psychologist, doctor or any other health professional who specializes in the management of negative thoughts.

Phil was able to manage his Saboteurs through coaching, training and his own hard work and focus. And, yes, he is now attacking his new business development activities with passion and zeal. Phil is now generating highly qualified clients through the focused networking and referral-building activities in his Booked Solid© Referral Marketing Plan and he has taken control of his future.

Before I say more about how Phil embarked upon his journey to rid or manage his Saboteurs, let's have a look at Francesca's story. Unlike Phil with his 20-year business, Francesca had yet to step into the "You are the Brand" world when I met her.

Francesca, the Corporate Refugee:

Francesca sought me out. She was worried. She had been in the corporate world for many years and had become very tired of it. She had recently purchased an engineering consulting business and failure was not an option. As a professional engineer, however, she had never been involved with sales at the large corporations where she had been employed. She had certainly never darkened the doors of the marketing department, nor taken part in any conversations that would serve to enlighten her on the topic. She felt like she was completely out of the loop.

Francesca was a widow with three children, two in university, and she had no time to lose. She could not wait the three to five years that her colleagues told her it would take to generate the revenue she needed.

And yet, Francesca was concerned about her own ability to market herself and to close business when she was in front of a prospect. She wondered how she was going to build her network and create referrals when she knew nothing about the process. She was also worried that she was not really a "people person."

In short, Francesca knew that she was ill-prepared for a perilous journey. And she asked her network about getting help. A member of my network was able to connect Francesca with me during a referral marketing program that I was delivering for the engineering association of which Francesca was a member. When Francesca and I met to review her situation, she shared with me her determination to acquire some new business development skills. And she wanted to start immediately.

I asked Francesca if she had the funds to support her family for the next year as she grew her networking, referral-building and sales-closing skills. Was she truly prepared for this journey? Francesca assured me that she was able to proceed. She had received an ample insurance settlement from her late husband's death, with which she had purchased the consulting business and she had set up a nest egg for her family.

I suggested to Francesca that if she needed more funds, there were many avenues available to her for alternate sources of financing. My network of business bankers, government-backed banks (known in Canada as BDC), mortgage specialists and factoring professionals was available to help her if and when she needed support.

I then asked her if she was willing to dedicate 20 hours a week to new business development for as long as she wanted to own her business. I reminded her that this dedication to the new business development process would be ongoing. Through the intensive training and coaching program I was going to set out for her, she would develop a mindset that would incorporate new business development activities into each and every day of her life. As she grew her new business development acumen, habits and plans, and developed the relationships that would serve her going forward, the results would follow. In the long run, Francesca would come to enjoy new business development. She would meet her goals and be a proud partner in business relationships that supported both her pocketbook and her soul.

I asked Francesca if she was ready to embrace this lifestyle of daily dedication to new business development. Did this look like it was something she could do, and did it sound like a good idea?

"Anything," she said, "Anything that will grow my business as quickly as possible."

Francesca and I agreed that she would join the Booked Solid Program which included weekly online classes on networking, referral-building and sales-closing strategies. Every two weeks, we would meet, just Francesca and I, for our coaching sessions, by phone or face-to-face. Our one-on-one coaching sessions were fundamental to Francesca's success. That time would allow us to assess, and start to address, the real enemy. Not the market. Not the competition. The Saboteurs. Francesca's Saboteurs.

Where did they lurk in Francesca? Some of them had already made themselves known through our conversation. And, of course, there were the inevitable ones, the 22 primary Saboteurs that most commonly lurk in the lives and minds of business professionals. The Saboteur Self-

Assessment (SSA) would tell the tale for both of us. We'll look at this tool in more detail later in the book, but if, like many of my clients, you just can't wait and *must* do your Saboteur Self-Assessment right now, please go to Chapter 3, entitled "Hell's Angels." The rest of you might want to join me in the following.

"Reproach of the Saboteurs"
What are the Saboteurs?

Well, a Saboteur, in the context of new business development and the business professional who offers their professional services, is a negative thought, or series of thoughts, that create a level of emotional discomfort for the business professional.

Depending on its intensity, this discomfort will have an impact on the business professional's confidence and, ultimately, their performance. And for those who have been victims of Saboteurs, and there are many, there is often little relief until they are silenced.

A Closer Look - The Saboteur Thought Spiral:
Here is an example of a nasty, yet common, Saboteur-related thought spiral:

Will I be able to build the customer base I need to support my new business? (The opening salvo)

Will I be able to create the relationships I require to generate referrals?

Do I have a lot of relationships?

Am I any good at making friends? (Oh oh!)

Do I have any friends?

Am I worthy of friends?

Am I worthy? (Ugh! Ouch!)

And so the business professional's thoughts move from their new business development plans to their deepest fears.

Where do these thoughts come from? Why do they surface with new business projects—when the business professional feels most vulnerable and needs that business to thrive?

These negative thoughts often bubble up from a business professional's unconscious mind, reminding them about unprocessed fears from earlier experiences. And masking many layers of self-limiting thoughts that are related to the same theme.

These thoughts started with a bad experience that has not been processed by the emotional memory of its owner. The solution? Unmasking the Saboteur by discovering the core issue at its heart. And exposing the fear that is supporting the entire Evil Saboteurial Empire.

Thoughts to Review:

- Do you have any Saboteurs lurking in the corners of your mind?
- Are these Saboteurs in your way?
- Ever thought about unpacking them?
- Do you think that this move will help grow your business?

A Note for Corporate Refugees

Francesca had been supported by a big brand for many years and she was going to have to make a crucial switch in mindset. As a "corporate refugee," she would need to learn about embracing her own brand, and leave all of the comforts and validation that a well-established brand provides to its employees and customers. Francesca was taking a huge leap and the Saboteurs would be looking for her. We needed to expose these Saboteurs as soon as possible, before they found her. Francesca's livelihood, and life, depended on it.

Phil and Francesca: What Happens When You Are the Brand?

Everyone has Saboteurs. Although we are rational beings, the human condition, by definition, includes negative thoughts. According to scientific research, approximately 70-80 per cent of our 50,000 daily thoughts are negative.

Seventy to 80 per cent! That's a lot of negative thoughts. And, yes, there are many places you can go with those negative thoughts. The secret to revenue success is to manage your Saboteurs. Especially at the times when you are most vulnerable, such as during major life events like:

- marriage, divorce or the death of a loved one;
- transitions of all kinds, including promotions, demotions, moving homes and the arrival of new family members and
- when you start or buy a new business or franchise.

All of these events represent change. Change challenges us. And while we are going through major change, we are creating a new world for ourselves. And that is not easy. As Prince Machiavelli would put it if he were in this conversation, "There is nothing more difficult to take in hand, more perilous to conduct, or more uncertain in its success, than to take the lead in the introduction of a new order of things."

When you become the brand, you are embracing more than a new business. You are "taking the lead in the introduction of a new order of things." You are creating a new entity: You as the brand.

In other words, you are relating to yourself in a way that you have never done before. Your fundamental relationship with yourself becomes different, as luck would have it, just as you are launching your business, wanting

28

and needing, so much, for it to be a success. You and your lifestyle are depending on it. It's a perfect storm of stress.

Thanks, a business professional might say, an identity crisis, when I least need it. It's true, and it's not fair. Here's the reality: You are now looking at yourself through the eyes of a customer and wondering, "Would I buy from me?" This can be a very uncomfortable question when you are just starting out on your own as a business professional and you are still forming your business proposition. The answer may well be, in all honesty, "No, I would not buy from me."

Why would you be coming up with such a negative and counterproductive answer about your own business?

Because you have yet to become the brand. There is a process that you must pursue. And it starts within you. You need to convince yourself that you *deserve* the business before you can convince prospects and your network.

Hurts = Saboteurs

A crucial consideration when confronting the Saboteurs is that many people have some outstanding, unprocessed "hurts" from long ago that have not been addressed and or resolved. These hurts can become the "Personal Saboteurs," the negative thoughts that arise from the wounds of childhood, discussed earlier in this chapter. For example, a child, Jimmy, was told both at school and at home that he did not sing well. So he stopped singing in spite of the fact that he really loved to sing.

As he grew older, Jimmy did not seek out opportunities to learn about music or pursue music as a hobby. Later on in Jimmy's life, this hurt manifested itself as a "Personal Saboteur," that had grown to the point where Jimmy was not able to share his message at all: even in adulthood, his voice was "not good enough."

We protect ourselves by burying these hurts. It's too overwhelming to deal with our wounds at once. So our subconscious mind "presents" these hurts when we are ready. Unfortunately, as time passes, these small hurts grow and expand, becoming generalized and dangerous Personal Saboteurs that can take us over and undermine our best intentions, as they did with Jimmy.

In times of transition and vulnerability, such as when you start your own business, and become the brand, all of your hurts and wounds become due. Or worse, overdue. It is as if all of your unprocessed pain becomes a collection of overdue bills which suddenly must be paid — now.

As you adopt an entirely new skin, that of the professional service provider who lives by your wits, your unresolved past doubts and insecurities bubble straight to the surface. Meanwhile, as a newly arrived business professional, you must put yourself out there every day, offering sound advice, wisdom and personality for the scrutiny of the entire marketplace; it can feel like a vulnerable place from which to operate. Your revenue is now directly tied to whether the personal skills you offer are accepted and valued by your prospects. The natural question to ask is, "Do I measure up?"

If we are harbouring old, unresolved hurts, we will more likely listen to that familiar negative voice that tells us that we're not good enough…for whatever reason. That Personal Saboteur will send us self-defeating messages that we very naturally listen to and allow to become self-fulfilling prophecies that hold us back from the very vision of success we crave. And so, clearly, we need to sort out these pains before we can move forward with confidence.

Two journalists, Katty Kay and Clare Shipman, recently studied the topic of confidence in their book, *The Confidence Code,* and concluded that, "Confidence is the stuff between moving our thoughts into action." If our thoughts are not entirely clear, it will have a direct impact on our confidence, and on our ability to demonstrate conviction to our network and, most of all, to ourselves.

Conviction = Results

The more confident you are, the more convincing you are. Greater conviction means stronger results.

What has come to fascinate me over my years of training and coaching business professionals is the exact precision of this equation. *Your inner world does matter, critically, to your business success.* Especially when you are the brand. In fact, I have come to the conclusion that there is a perfect relationship between *how* you are feeling about yourself and the *results* that you see in your business, and your brand.

Assume that you are a confident business professional, firing on all pistons, with very few Saboteurs. You are at 94.2 per cent of your potential. Your business results will directly reflect that 94.2 per cent and you will enjoy revenue levels that are 94.2 per cent of your potential.

Unfortunately, as I discovered with my clients and with my own experience, this equation also holds true when you turn the prism and things are not going well for you, internally. If you have suffered a personal blow like a divorce or sad life event, or you are suffering from low energy due to diet or burnout, your business results will provide a mirror to your inner world.

In reality, working with only 59.5 per cent of your full personal potential turns out revenue results that are 59.5 per cent of your real potential. Ouch! Earning 60 per cent of your planned revenue for the year is not exactly what you signed up for when you started your business or practice. And that 40 per cent drop in earnings will only add or create new problems. As a result, many of my clients are miserable by the time they make the decision to work with me. They need help with their Saboteurs as soon as possible.

I decided that it was time to expose these Saboteurs, and identify the damage that they were wreaking on the mindsets of business professionals. That's when I started to write about the Saboteurs in my Monday Morning Referral Tips, isolating the real impact of the Saboteurs on all business professionals. They had created hell for their hosts and it was time for their cruelty to be exposed.

Let's go deeper into the private hell that so many, too many, business professionals experience when they are creating their own revenue.

YOU ARE THE BRAND: THE HELL OF IT ALL

There are many damaging assumptions about new business development, one of the most destructive of which is "Anyone can promote their own business."

Business professionals invest many years developing their accreditations, and one would think that this would be enough to prove their own worth to themselves. And yet it's been my experience, time and again, that they're the toughest audience they will ever have to face.

Ouch! It just does not seem fair. At the same time, it does bear noting that we are a vulnerable species. Remember that I mentioned that approximately 80 per cent of our average 50,000 thoughts per day are negative? Research into brain function determines that this negative mindset starts with our parents' daily messages to keep ourselves safe. It makes sense that those messages largely comprise "Don'ts" and "Stops" as we grow into our ability to take care of ourselves.

We can become heavily imprinted with these ongoing, fundamentally negative messages. And negative thoughts can attract more negative thoughts. This is a ripe harvest for the Saboteurs and can become severe enough to immobilize the professional as they attempt to follow through on their new client development activities. Our subconscious focus is on avoiding pain, rather than creating pleasure.

It's understandable for any business professional to lack confidence in their ability to promote themselves and develop new business: most of us have very little training or coaching in the all-important process of creating clients for themselves.

Networking, referral-building, even closing for consulting contracts are skills that are not taught in traditional professional schools. And these key survival skills are not developed formally within academic business-school environments, either. In fact, most professional and academic institutions regard "selling" with considerable disdain.

So that leaves most of us with the training our parents provided, which usually represents a fairly meagre contribution to our skill set in the area. This is especially problematic if our parents frequently gave us negative messages that we perceived as "hurts" that ultimately blossomed into Personal Saboteurs.

Yikes! No wonder business professionals are frightened about new business development.

And what happens when you add to the mix the fear of making a mistake? Or of being overly "salesy" with treasured members of your network? And throw in one or two of the insecurities to which we all fall prey, just for good measure. Let's see -- no training, a confusing amount of social disdain for the selling world, considerable social risk and personal insecurity. We have the perfect soil in which the Saboteurs can germinate, don't we?

And, worst of all, the Saboteurs play at the most critical, vulnerable time—while the business professional must find his or her way.

Thoughts to Review

- Do I recognize any of Phil's or Francesca's pain in my world?
- Do I have Saboteurs?
- Do they get in my way?
- Am I comfortable being the brand for my business?
- If not, what do I want to do about it?

Chapter 2:

The Impact of the Saboteurs on Your Health and Well-Being: The Biological View

I was very concerned about Joe. He was worried about his business and he had every reason to be apprehensive. His revenue was down and his bills were mounting. His confidence was low and he was not feeling well. He was in no position to cope with his situation.

Joe had not been sleeping, and that had been the case for several weeks. He was punch-drunk with exhaustion and not able to move forward until he was able to get some rest. His lack of energy was holding him back. I told Joe that I would be happy to help him with his new business development challenges—when he had some sleep under his belt. I asked him to go to his doctor and discuss solutions for getting some rest. Go figure, I said to myself, I'm advising Joe his best new business development strategy is to get some sleep.

Body First:
There is not a lot that anyone can do to help you grow your revenue if you are not operating at full steam. You can't see the "big picture" view of what's going on in your business and you trip on the details. You need all of your native energy—and more. When the Saboteurs are present and taking over your positive mindset, they have a real impact on your inner landscape, and, just as significantly, on your physical well-being.

We all recognize that our bodies feel uncomfortable when we are not handling our world with grace and ease. My friend and colleague, Dr. Laura Crawford, is a highly respected naturopath who has spent years studying the physiological bases for stress; she sheds a very bright light on the real impact the Saboteurs have on our bodies.

Dr. Laura reminds us that we need to maintain a "Body First" attitude. If we want to keep our businesses in good shape, and avoid the problems that come with burnout, we need to make sure that we take care of ourselves first. With our physical bodies in high gear, we can marshal the strength needed to recognize and fight off the Saboteurs.

Dr. Laura Crawford, ND, on the Saboteurs and Our "Lizard Brain":

The Saboteurs are negative thought patterns that deflate your self-esteem and hold you back from what it is that you are trying to accomplish. Generally, these voices engage in a lot of negative self-talk that makes you feel badly about yourself or a situation and that keep you from seeing how you can take action.

Curiously, the Saboteurs are created out of love and out of protection. They are trying to ensure your safety by making sure that you don't stand out so that you can't fail. They maintain the status quo, which on an evolutionary level ensures safety and survival. Unfortunately, if you are trying to better yourself or your business, this process is maladaptive. To truly understand the Saboteurs and the effects that they have on your business, and your health, we must first understand the part of the brain that they target and are created from, the amygdala.

The amygdala, an almond-shaped structure within the brain, is also known as the Lizard Brain. This is because it essentially has the same processing power as the brain found in a lizard. This is no longer sufficient in the modern-day business world.

Think of the goals of a lizard. It is unlikely that you will see them making strategic business decisions and they are not known for their intricate social relationships. The primary ambition of a lizard is survival. As Seth Godin says, "The lizard brain is hungry, scared, angry, and horny."

At the root of the lizard brain are the emotions of anger and fear, and at the root of the Saboteurs are the same emotions. The fear does not have to be legitimate. It feels "real" if your body can sense it and it can be traced to your outside circumstances or your internal experience. Your beliefs, your actions and your experience of the world can all create justification for the presence of the Saboteurs.

This fear is based on a sense of danger. Humans used to recognize danger when we were foraging for our survival—while being chased by a predator, for example. In the 21st century, we are hounded instead by countless emails, meetings and an infinite amount of technological clutter that can abruptly interrupt our day. Our body, however, responds the same way it would if there were a real physical threat.

The amygdala is responsible for many functions relating to fear. It is used in interpreting facial expressions, it can re-frame memories based on the emotions associated with an experience and it can condition your body to have a very specific fear response.

Have you ever met anyone who seemed to view every situation as a catastrophe, regardless of the reality of the situation? The trained pessimist who "knew" that everything was going to go wrong, that the meeting did not go well and that the sky was going to fall? If you are around these people on a regular basis you can almost watch them spiral down into a black hole of noisy catastrophe. These people have very poorly trained amygdalas. They not only respond to danger, but also create danger in their minds. This is hard on relationships, and it keeps them from meeting their potential.

Our lizard brain, when allowed to run amuck, can create panic. If the Saboteurs and the thoughts of the lizard brain are not leashed they can have a snowball effect, until the person feels completely overwhelmed and alone.

This fear response was originally meant to support our survival. We had to survive against real danger, not just perceived danger. Think about it, when we were hunter-gatherers we would be out in the woods picking berries to eat when all of a sudden we would come up against a predator, such as a bear. Our bodies had to bypass the thought process and just act.

In a philosophical sense, we could see the bear, hear the bear and feel the terror of encountering it. We could wonder if the bear was hungry and might actually attack, and then map out an escape route. By the time we would have finished that thought process we would be lunchmeat.

Instead, the amygdala senses or sees the bear and immediately calls your body to act. Your heart begins to race so that it can pump more blood to your muscles. Your vision narrows and becomes crisper so that you can acutely see where you need to go, and your muscles become tighter so that you have extra speed and strength to get away.

Your body also shuts off some processes that are not necessary in that scenario. Digestive function is halted, there is a relative decrease in hearing, and sexual response is inhibited. That makes sense. In a survival situation you do not want to put your energy towards digestion, and you certainly do not have time for sex.

Your body also shuts down the part of your brain that brings logic and reason to situations. Blood is diverted away from the area of our brain that allows us to think rationally and moves towards the amygdala, so that we can just act, and to the muscles, so we can run. When a bear is chasing us, this is great. The musings of the rational part of our brain don't impede our process with thoughts like, "Will I actually be able to run away?"

All of these processes are completely appropriate for survival, but in our current business world our perception of danger relates less to a physical threat and more to the stress of a full inbox, the challenges of client management and a raft of impending deadlines.

In our current business world, there is no recovery time. The emails don't end, the meetings become more frequent and our "to do" list piles up. In fact, in many companies the better you are, the more responsibility you are given. At least when we were up against a bear we knew we would be safe for a little while once we escaped the immediate threat of disaster. Our body could recover, and we could rest up for the next brush with danger... But what if we stay stuck in a state of stress response?

The Health Effects of the Saboteurs:

The Saboteurs trigger a stress response within the body, otherwise known as fight or flight. Evolution designed this so that when we experience danger, we fight that danger: we engage in a duel, or run away. Three specific phases of stress have an impact on both the body and the brain and they are Alarm, Resistance and Burnout.

Stage One: The Alarm Phase:

The alarm phase of the stress response is responsible for supporting us during short-term stressors. For example, when we decide to go for a run our body will release cortisol and adrenaline, two stress hormones. This allows our heart to pump stronger and deliver more blood to our tissues and it helps us focus on the task at hand. This is a positive stress and a healthy response. When we complete the task we get a rush of hormones that makes us feel a sense of accomplishment. There is a sense of closure and we get a chance to recover. We feel in control of our environment and more open to encounters with other people. When we take on more challenges we have more confidence, as we feel qualified to complete them successfully. However, when this phase becomes prolonged and we feel many stressors piling up on one another, our bodies will move into what is called the resistance phase.

Stage Two: The Resistance Phase:

The resistance phase of stress is where our resiliency is challenged and our attitudes about stress affect our physical response to it. For example, if you believe stress to be a positive challenge, your body and heart release the same chemicals that they would when you experience joy. This protects the heart and allows you to experience longer periods of stress with no negative physical consequences.

If, however, you view the stressors as threats, pressures or negative demands, then your body's ability to cope is compromised. Fatigue begins to set in, your memory starts to suffer and your immune system's efficiency decreases. Emotionally, you may start to feel irritable and anxious, sounds might bother you more than normal and your view of the world around you might be somewhat distorted. People around you might perceive that you are impatient. Your body adapts to these demands by releasing more sugars and fats to give you more energy and stamina, as a predictable result, however, blood sugar and cholesterol issues start to show up in your blood work. Finally, your sleep starts to suffer, compounding all of the above issues and making it harder for your body and mind to recover.

Many people can spend months or even years at this stage; however, at some point, the body will move into the exhaustion stage. If you have any unidentified Saboteurs at work in your life, your physical issues will be compounded.

Phase Three: Exhaustion or Burnout

The exhaustion phase is akin to burnout. The cortisol that was released to keep you alert and awake dwindles, and your body and mind become exhausted from the never-ending stress. The earlier warning signs begin to transform into major problems. Focus and concentration suffer. Emotionally, you may find yourself imbalanced across the spectrum, moving through various stages of anxiety, anger, and depression or hopelessness. Because the physical effects of all of the other stages of stress are compounded you may start to move into a disease state during this stage. Diagnoses such as high blood pressure, heart disease, ulcers, strokes, rashes and skin issues, migraines, infertility and gastrointestinal issues may all be markers of exhaustion.

The interesting thing is that some of the symptoms of stress can actually trigger the Saboteurs to further run rampant. The body and mind are intricately connected, so when you experience physical symptoms your mind will try to find a reason, regardless of whether it is an accurate one. Our body's own stress response starts creating a playground for the Saboteurs.

Consider this, you are about to go into a meeting to give a pitch to a company that is interested in purchasing your service or product. You haven't eaten all morning since you have been doing last-minute preparations and naturally your blood sugar starts to drop. You become shaky with heart palpitations and your level of focus wanes. You didn't think that you were worried about this proposal; you knew it was going to be a slam-dunk, but now you are starting to wonder if you are actually more nervous than you thought. Your mind starts racing, trying to sort out why you might be "stressed." You focus on the small details of what might go wrong, rather than the big picture of what a great job you're going to do. Now, instead of going into your pitch thinking of it as a sure thing, you have created a hundred reasons why it won't work out or why you aren't good enough. In fact, it doesn't matter if you found a hundred reasons; just one is enough to sabotage all of your efforts.

It does not have to be this way. Deepak Chopra says that we know 98 per cent of what we will do tomorrow. It is our habits and our emotions that determine our behaviour. Sometimes changing our tomorrow requires us to do things *differently than we did yesterday. Once you understand why you feel and react a certain way, you have the ability to change it." – Dr. Laura*

Let's Change Our Tomorrow:

So there's the rub of it all. We need to understand "why we feel and react a certain way." Then, and only then, do we have the ability to change it. As Dr. Laura so succinctly puts it, your lizard brain will rule you, if you let it. And then it feeds on your reactions, creating even more Saboteurs to plague your world.

And look at all of the devastating effects of exhaustion on your body that Dr. Laura describes: high blood pressure, heart disease, ulcers, strokes, rashes and skin issues, migraines, infertility and gastrointestinal issues. Is harbouring the Saboteurs worth it? I think not. Their presence in your life can threaten your life. And the health of your business. Dr. Laura will return in Chapter 7, The Antidotes to the Saboteurs, to provide a cornucopia of smart solutions to help us be at our "physical" best. The Saboteurs are challenged to find a home in a robust, healthy and happy body.

Thoughts to Review:

- Do I have any of the symptoms that Dr. Laura describes?
- Am I getting enough sleep?
- Is it time to understand why I feel and react a certain way?
- What is my lizard brain doing to my body?
- Am I concerned about its impact on my body
- Do I want to change my current situation?

Chapter 3:
Hell's Angels: Saboteur Self-Assessment Tool

I was running down from my college dining room into the beautiful old house that was my university residence. I was at the end of my third year; I had four essays due within a five-day period. Plus I was directing a play, I was a student leader and I had, shall we say, a complicated social life. And I had no idea what my future would hold. Unbeknownst to me, I was way off the stress scale.

Suddenly, I could not breathe. I was completely disoriented, frightened out of my mind, with no physical reason for my panic. The shock of it all stopped me completely in my tracks. I was terrified. What was happening to me?

What was happening to me? My demons had taken me by storm. They had literally immobilized me. And so I experienced the frightening condition that gripped my world for far too long. It helped to learn the many names for this condition: ennui, disquiet, panic attacks or anxiety. I will never forget that day, the day that I felt the power of my inner demons. The Saboteurs had introduced themselves, painfully, to my world.

When wrestling with your own devils, your Saboteurs, it is important to understand the nature of their game. As Dr. Laura puts it in Chapter 2, it is key to know that "Our lizard brain, when allowed to run amuck, can create panic. If the Saboteurs and the thoughts of the lizard brain are not leashed they can have a snowball effect until the person feels completely overwhelmed and alone."

As you will observe from my own story, I have experienced those moments of feeling overwhelmed and alone. I have also heard my clients describe those awful moments—many times. A few clients have asked me to "talk them off the edge."

The famous Napoleon Hill quote from *Think and Grow Rich*, "What the mind of man can conceive and believe, it can achieve," sounds ominous in the context of the angst of the business professional that is under this sort of stress. You can almost smell the desperation of some business professionals — trapped between their Saboteurs and their need to move forward. Ouch!

Self-doubt, second-guessing, self-sabotage are all gifts of the human condition, a by-product of our complex brain, which encompasses our lizard brain as well as our most sophisticated reflective selves. These intellectual parts all come with the blessing of the ability to reason. Our capacity to take a bird's eye view of the situation and manage these so-called "gifts" has a lot to do with our ability to succeed and to be happy.

Whether there is an Olympic gold medal, the Stanley Cup, Wimbledon or a casual basketball game on the line, our inner game determines whether we win or lose. It is no surprise that the concept of coaching, which helps us so much with the management of our thoughts, along with our Saboteurs, germinated in the modern sports world first.

Tim Gallwey's book, *The Inner Game of Tennis*, published in 1974, highlighted the role of psychology in creating a state of peak performance. He stated that the opponent in one's head was greater than the one on the other side of the net. Business professionals must likewise manage their "inner game," when they embark upon the

"You are the brand" journey. They need to develop many skills, maintain them at an elite performance level at all times, and, most important of all, manage all of their doubts and fears, don't they?

There is no difference between a business professional and an athlete when it comes to the *importance* of maintaining their skills for as long as the game is on. The difference between the business professional and an athlete, however, is that the skills that business professionals are required to foster lie in the area of new business development. How can you best manage your inner game when you are the brand? The fundamental step to managing *any* inner game is to manage your Saboteurs.

This section of the book is designed to help you with that considerable task. The task of defining and cataloguing your Saboteurs, giving them names and cages, will prepare you for the next step of your long, continuous new business development journey. As Dr. Laura puts it, you must "leash" the Saboteurs before moving forward and there is a cost associated with not doing so.

Not Naming the Enemy:

We know that businesses fail at jaw-dropping rates. Especially within the first two years. In fact, the failure rate of businesses is even higher than the failure rate of marriages.

To quote small business expert, Tim Carroll, from an article on small business in The Business Insider, "Small business failure rates vary depending on where the statistics are coming from, [but] generally 50 to 70 per cent fail within the first 18 months."

(Source:http://www.businessinsider.com/small-business-owners-are-optimistic-2013-6)

Compare these figures to the Canadian divorce rate cited by Statistics Canada, "Fluctuating between 35% and 42%, the proportion of marriages projected to end in divorce has remained relatively stable in the last 20 years. (Source:http://well-being.esdc.gc.ca/misme-iowb/.3ndic.1t.4r@-eng.jsp?iid=76)

In 2008, 40.7% of marriages were projected to end in divorce before the thirtieth wedding anniversary."

A 50 to 70 per cent failure rate in 18 months for small businesses compared to a 40.7 per cent failure rate in 30 years for marriages! Go figure — people are better at running their marriages than running their businesses. Why is there such a high failure rate for businesses? There are many possible answers to that question. A recent study of 12,000 successful business professionals found that 91.4 per cent attributed their business success to networking. Could the high failure rate of businesses, then, be tied to a lack of referrals, a lack of networking? Or could the high failure rate of businesses be tied to something else? Are there other barriers to business success? And could these barriers also be found within, right between the ears of, the business professional and within their own mindset?

Throughout my years of coaching and training business professionals around the world, I have come to realize that the real battles occur internally, within the hearts and minds of the business professionals themselves, rather than out there in the marketplace. In other words, shut down the inner debilitating voices, develop networking, referral-building and sales closing skills, create a solid message and a full activity plan, with reinforcement training and coaching, and the day will be won in the outer world. And the referrals will come marching in.

Before that happy day can arrive, the patterns that feed those horrible destructive voices within the business owner must be unearthed, exposed for their true negative impact and managed so that the business professional can move forward boldly into their new world, avoiding as many problems as possible . Then, and only then, can the fundamental networking, referral-building and sales strategy training do their valuable work and change the business professional's life and those that care for him or her. Forever. In other words, only once this internal "noble struggle" has occurred, can training "stick" and success march within reach.

What is the nature of these debilitating patterns, these negative stories that business professionals carry within their own heads? Why are they so powerful that they limit success and prevent people from forming the type of relationships that will nourish their businesses?

Naming the enemy, the Saboteurs, is the key to managing them. Once you have expunged or managed your Saboteurs, you can create a "green field" in your mind which will foster the right environment for all of the new learning that you require to create your own revenue.

To help with the process of naming, and caging, your Saboteurs, I have developed a diagnostic instrument called The Saboteur Self-Assessment Tool. The objective of this exercise is to help you define the types of Saboteurs that have settled into your mind. Once you have named your Saboteurs, you will have a handle on the type of Saboteurs that are plaguing you. The Saboteurs become the symptoms that lead to the cure. You can then move on to the next step of caging the Saboteurs, and managing them, and rescue your life and business from their evil influence.

Your Saboteur Self-Assessment:
How Are Saboteurs Affecting Your Inner Game?

Please circle the number that best identifies your experience with the following statements. 1= Never   2 = Not often   3= Sometimes   4 = Often   5= Always

I like being in a sales role	1	2	3	4	5
My self-talk about new business development is positive	1	2	3	4	5
I embrace rejection in new business development	1	2	3	4	5
Opportunities in new business development excite me	1	2	3	4	5
I see abundance everywhere	1	2	3	4	5
I always move forward when I need to	1	2	3	4	5
I bounce back easily when challenged	1	2	3	4	5
I feel good about myself	1	2	3	4	5
I enjoy my relationship with money	1	2	3	4	5
I always ask for the true value of my services	1	2	3	4	5

I enjoy networking	1	2	3	4	5
I think that people will give me a referral	1	2	3	4	5
I refer other people	1	2	3	4	5
I believe that networking works	1	2	3	4	5
I am comfortable walking into a room full of people	1	2	3	4	5
I like meeting new people	1	2	3	4	5
I like small talk	1	2	3	4	5
I know what to do if I give a bad referral	1	2	3	4	5
I know what to do if I receive a bad referral	1	2	3	4	5
I am adequately organized to follow up	1	2	3	4	5
I work with my ideal client	1	2	3	4	5
I have the personality for networking	1	2	3	4	5

Your Score: A Quick Word

The statements above represent 22 activities or attitudes that are fundamental to creating revenue, specifically by referrals. If you answered 1 "never," 2 "not often" or 3 "sometimes" it is possible that you will have challenges with implementing actions that are tied to that principle. For example, if you answered "sometimes" to the statement, "I like being in a sales role," you could be open to the "I Hate Sales" Sales Saboteur since you have not entirely embraced the new business development or sales role in your business. If you responded with 4, "often," or 5, "always," to the same statement, it is likely that you have embraced the sales role in your business.

The Saboteur Self-Assessment Tool is designed to provide you with a yardstick for evaluating the extent to which you are able to manage your negative thoughts regarding new business development.

There is no high or low mark, no winners or losers. There is just you, and feedback on any thoughts about new business development that may or may not serve you.

Thoughts to Review

- Do I have any negative thoughts about my business?
- Do these thoughts get in the way of my success?
- Can I identify a pattern?
- Is it possible that I have Saboteurs?
- Did I respond with 1, 2, or 3 to any statements in the Saboteur Self-Assessment Tool?
- Would I like to learn more about some of my Saboteurs?
- Do I want to get rid of my Saboteurs?

Chapter 4:
The Fatal Duo: The Two Categories of Saboteurs

GIVING YOUR SABOTEURS NAMES AND CAGES:

Now that you have isolated your Saboteurs with the help of the Saboteur Self-assessment (SSA) tool in Chapter 3, you can proceed to the defining and cataloguing stage of understanding them. This will ultimately help you to confine them in "cages" and find workable solutions for the problems they cause. In Chapters 5 and 6 we will name and explore in detail the 22 Saboteurs turned up by the SSA tool in Chapter 3, but first let's look at the two main types of Saboteurs so we can begin the "caging" process.

It may surprise you that the mere act of naming, or identifying, your Saboteurs will help you. It's true. The very fact that your Saboteurs, your self-limiting thoughts, have been exposed for you to scrutinize and challenge is very valuable. They can no longer hide in your unconscious mind and they can no longer ambush you. You might even be able to anticipate the situations under which they might visit you. And experience fewer surprise attacks by your lizard brain.

For many years, I have observed the numerous "head challenges" that present themselves within the inner landscapes of my clients. And, of course, I have experienced the Saboteurs personally in relation to my own new business development activities. While the list of Saboteurs may never be complete (human misery does not allow for that), it certainly provides a comprehensive foundation covering most of the key Saboteurs and obstacles you may encounter.

I designed the Saboteur Self-Assessment (SSA) Tool to assist with the cataloguing or "caging" of the Saboteurs. The tool, and therefore this book, classifies the 22 Saboteurs I've identified here into two very broad categories:

1. **The Sales Saboteurs:** Saboteurs that develop from flawed assumptions about new business development. Statements 1-10 address these Saboteurs.

2. **The Networking/Referral Saboteurs:** Saboteurs that develop from unrealistic expectations and lack of training on the topics of networking and building referrals. Statements 11-21 address these Saboteurs.

All of the saboteurs in these two categories prevent you from doing what you really need to do to sustain a consistent flow of referrals and new business. Any one of these Saboteurs can result in (sometimes severely) limited productivity for even the most talented of business professionals. Before we move on to the detailed process of naming all the Saboteurs individually in the next chapters, it's important to understand a little bit about the broader categories into which they all fall. The more you understand about how the Saboteurs develop and function, the better equipped you will be to defeat them.

THE SALES SABOTEURS

The Sales Saboteurs develop from the uncritical adoption of the many myths about new business development that exist in our society. From the pathetic salesman, Willy Loman, in Arthur Miller's book ***Death of a Salesman***, to the fast-talkin', swashbucklin' Jordan Belfort in the movie ***Wolf of Wall Street***, the public has been exposed to consistently negative images of people in sales roles.

Salespeople are almost always portrayed in roles where they appear to be manipulative, self-interested, amoral or immoral, and certainly abusive of the public trust. As a result, salespeople are generally disrespected or dismissed by the disappointed public. In a recent study in the US of the public's trust of selected professions, salespeople were rated right at the bottom of the trust list, along with attorneys and politicians.

From the days of the selling of snake oil from wagons in the late 1800s, to the door-to-door Fuller brush men of the 1950s, and onwards to the automobile salespeople of today, untrained and desperate salespeople have continued to offend their prospects and reluctant customers with the abrasive and insensitive management of their relationships. Some have had inappropriate ideas of what a proper "balance of power" is in a sales relationship and others have been so focused on their sales targets that they have neglected to take care of the customer.

While there may be notable exceptions, the public perception remains the same: if you are selling anything, you are not to be trusted.

The impact of this negative view of salespeople is devastating for those who are suddenly tarred with the "sales" brush when they offer their personal services. They fear that, to their friends and family and, worst of all, within their own minds, they will become that person who is not to be trusted. And the Saboteurs have their way as you, the unsuspecting business professional, attempt to separate your feelings of self from the image of the wide-spread perception of the powerful and overbearing loud-mouthed salesperson.

Were some of your answers in Statements 1-10 of the Saboteur Self-Assessment in the 1, 2, or 3 slots? These response levels might suggest that you have been hosting some Sales Saboteurs.

Sales Saboteurs are inevitable in a world where the role of the salesperson does not come with validation or respect. In Chapter 5, we will pursue the individual Sales Saboteurs that you have identified in your personal assessment.

THE REFERRAL SABOTEURS

Networking appears to be the "silver bullet" for all successful people. From building job opportunities, to creating referrals, to success in life and love, we are told that networking is what it is all about. This is a very general term for a lot of activities, with lots of myths and misunderstandings about what will really work. And yet there are not many places to learn about this mysterious business practice called networking. You will not find much formal training on networking in the curricula of business schools or community colleges.

I remember when I was learning Marketing 101 early in my business career, I noticed there were very specific parameters and systems to support the various methods of new business development. They included advertising, public relations and even cold calling (the web had not arrived). "Word of mouth" was added to the list as an afterthought as if this negligible activity were hardly worth our time.

So we find ourselves in a conundrum. We are asked to embrace the importance of networking and developing referrals while receiving precious little information that

54

would help us "how" we do this important life-defining activity. And we are definitely not provided with any system or details on strategies that would support our networking efforts so we can avoid mistakes.

As is the case when there are a lot of perceptions, and very little opportunity for education, there is a huge abyss that is filled with insecurity and uncertainty, ripe for the growth of all kinds of Saboteurs.

Were some of your answers in Statements 11- 22 of the Saboteur Self-Assessment in the 1, 2, or 3 categories? These response levels might suggest that you have been hosting some Referral Saboteurs. Chapter 6 will outline 12 Referral Saboteurs in more detail.

CONCLUSION:

In Chapter 4 we explored two broad categories of Saboteurs that commonly inhabit the mindset of the unsuspecting business professional: The Sales Saboteurs as well as The Referral Saboteurs. Organizing the Saboteurs into these two main groups is designed to assist all business professionals with their self-assessment process.

By completing the self-assessment in Chapter 3, which facilitates the "naming" process, along with the cataloguing of the two types of Saboteurs in Chapter 4, which enables the "caging" process, you can start the critical path to vanquishing your Saboteurs.

The Beginning of the End of the Saboteurs
The "naming" process is the beginning of the end of the Saboteurs. Saboteurs enjoy the murky world of confusion and fear; this environment allows them to grow

ever stronger. They do not like the definition that comes with the naming of their activities. Once there is a spotlight on their particularly insidious hold on anyone's world, it is more difficult for the Saboteurs to have their way with the delicate inner workings of a business professional.

As soon as the Saboteurs are named, there is an opportunity to wrestle them to the ground and to place them into their cages, where they truly belong. In Chapter 7, "The Antidotes to the Saboteurs," we will explore the variety of tools you can use to manage or destroy them, while giving you an overall sense of how powerful this task can be.

In the meantime, by exploring the two categories of Saboteurs, you can identify your own inner demons for their possible future destruction. The battle now begins, in earnest. Are you ready?

Thoughts to Review:

- What types of Saboteurs do I have?

- Can I identify a trend in my Saboteurs? Do they tend to fall into the sales or the networking/referral category? Or am I afflicted with both?

- Do I want to learn more about my Saboteurs?

- Do I want to do anything about them?

Chapter 5:
The Sales Saboteurs

I was in my early twenties in the mid 1970s and I was thrilled to have my own car. I could not believe it. I was a recent university graduate, and I already had my own brand-ne-e-w, sky blu-u-e, Monte Carlo. I was so proud of myself and I felt that my career was really moving forward. I'd been given a job as the salesperson for Liquid Paper in the Ottawa area, Canada's capital, and to support my activities, I had been given a company car. (Did I mention it was sky blue?)

My friends were excited for me and shared my new status with three of my university professors.

"Oh, dear," they said to my friends, "Paula has become a sales rep. That's too bad."

It was the first time that I would hear of the stigma around salespeople. Unfortunately, I was going to hear about this stigma for the rest of my life. I have often joked at speaking events that I am going to dedicate my life to getting rid of the dishonour that swirls around the sales profession, my punch line being that I intend to live until I am 150 years old.

Almost everyone has a story about how a really insensitive salesperson turned them off when they were making a major purchase, such as a car or a house. These stories make it appear as though there are sleazy salespeople in every car dealership. Some car companies run ads that play on these negative experiences and state that consumers will have a much better experience, and feel better tended, at their dealership. Negative attitudes towards salespeople are everywhere and so it is not surprising that the Sales Saboteurs are likely to rear their ugly heads, in whole or in part, when business professionals become responsible for new business development within their own firms. Or when they put up a shingle with their name, and reputation, on it. When they become the brand.

Business professionals do not want to be associated with these nasty, negative stereotypes of salespeople. Their fear of being associated with this group grows quickly, even as their dependence on building sales and generating their own business revenue becomes more important to their financial picture.

Exposing, or "naming" these Sales Saboteurs is the best way for you to start to move forward, and away from the dangerous impact of these negative images on your confidence. We will explore each of the 22 Saboteurs and explain the reasons for their existence in Chapter 6, "The Sales Saboteurs" and Chapter 7, "The Referral Saboteurs."

Evaluating Your Score: A Longer Word:

Each of the Saboteurs in the Self-Assessment (SSA) tool, which we saw earlier in Chapter 3, has been matched with a statement. If you scored a 1, 2 or 3 ("never," "not often" or "sometimes") on Statements # 1-10 of the tool , you will want to look more deeply into the details I've provided in this chapter about what that might mean to your revenue. Every Assessment Statement relates to a specific Sales Saboteur.

For example, if you rated Statement #1, "I Love Selling My Services," with 1 "never," 2 "not often" or 3 "sometimes," you may want to read more about Saboteur # 1, the "I Hate Selling" Sales Saboteur.

If you rated Statement # 5, "I See Abundance Everywhere," with 1 "never," 2 "not often" or 3 "sometimes," you may want to read more about Saboteur # 5, the "Scarcity" Sales Saboteur.

If you scored a 4 "often" or 5 "always" to any of the #1–10 Sales Saboteur statements, you can congratulate yourself on resisting the Saboteur that corresponds to the statement number. At the same time, you may still want to learn more about that Saboteur to make sure that you will recognize it if it presents itself to you, or a member of your network, in the future. With the Saboteurs, knowledge is always power.

The List of Sales Saboteurs: Statements #1–10

Saboteur #1 – The "I Hate Selling" Sales Saboteur
Saboteur #2 – The "I Have Negative Self-Talk About Business Development" Sales Saboteur
Saboteur #3 – The "Fear of Rejection" Sales Saboteur
Saboteur #4 – The "Fears Sales" Sales Saboteur
Saboteur #5 – The "Scarcity" Sales Saboteur
Saboteur #6 – The "Procrastination" Sales Saboteur
Saboteur #7 – The "Lack of Resilience" Sales Saboteur
Saboteur #8 – The "Lack of Self-Esteem" Sales Saboteur
Saboteur #9 – The "Money" Sales Saboteur
Saboteur #10 – The "True Value of Services" Sales Saboteur

SABOTEUR # 1:
THE "I HATE SELLING" SALES SABOTEUR

Statement #1: "I love selling my services" Never? Not Often? Sometimes?

Many people who have minimal sales experience don't like selling because they do not want to be associated with the negative perceptions of salespeople. These unfortunate attitudes have a real impact on their willingness to embrace new business development, especially in the critical daily activities that generate opportunities for creating new clients.

Saboteur # 1, the "I Hate Selling" Sales Saboteur, reviews this attitude and offers the number-one solution to this Saboteur: education. When you boil down the sales function and consider its true contribution, that is, to "manage relationships," the simple reality of this role becomes more obvious. The buyer has a need and the salesperson meets that need with a service or product. Take away the sleaze and snake oil perceptions that come with the Sales Saboteurs and you will have a very basic exchange of goods or services to satisfy human needs. Isn't it time to manage our attitudes accordingly?

One of the saddest business moments in all my years of mentoring sales professionals came early in my life as a sales and marketing executive.

A promising young man had joined our company and he shared with me that he deeply regretted his new role as a sales professional. He worried that he would always feel unsuccessful as he had become "just a salesman." That same week a colleague in our industry, for whose business acumen I had considerable respect, told me that he had said to his son, "Don't you grow up and become a sales manager like your old man—make something of yourself."

Both men went on to have very successful sales careers and make a lot of money. Sadly, both men never felt successful in spite of the fact that they really enjoyed their work. Why didn't they feel successful? Because of the stigma of being in sales. The truth of the matter is that there is generally not a high regard for salespeople in our society. And yet, we respect wealth — very much. But not the key activity that creates wealth. How does wealth happen? Well, usually, something is sold. By someone. *So we are in a system that has no respect for the people who drive the engine of our wealth.* It is one of our biggest, and most damaging, social contradictions.

With this massive bias, imagine the amount of confusion, negativity, and even shame, felt by most business professionals as they prepare to do new business development for their organizations or for their own business. *Overnight,* they are faced with one of society's most limiting and contradictory beliefs. *Overnight,* they see themselves as the sleazy salesperson they have always despised.

How did this happen? How did the generators of wealth become the lowest men and women on the totem pole? And what to do? What to *do*? As is often the case, it is education that sets us free. All of the individuals who offer services or products—that is, who sell something—need to be trained, just like any other professional or tradesperson. By creating a system and a process for their new business development plans, trained salespeople and business professionals can build and manage the trust of their clients to create a win-win for both parties. In this way, business professionals can free themselves of crippling beliefs and learn to develop productive and authentic relationships that are fair and respectful to them and their clients.

Thoughts to Review:

- What are my beliefs about salespeople?
- Do these beliefs affect my comfort and confidence when I am offering my own services to my prospects?
- Do I feel that it might help with my success to have another look at my beliefs about sales people?

SABOTEUR #2: "I HAVE NEGATIVE SELF-TALK ABOUT NEW BUSINESS DEVELOPMENT"

Statement #2: "My self-talk is positive about new business development" Never? Not often? Sometimes?

The daily pursuit of new business development activities is the key to creating new clients for your business or practice. It is that simple. If you dedicate three or four hours every day to the right new business development activities you will generate the revenue that will build the lifestyle of your dreams.

In order to achieve this daily routine, which is the basic mindset of every successful business professional, you must rid yourself of negative self-talk about sales and the sales role. Saboteur # 2, the "I Have Negative Self-Talk about New Business Development Saboteur," discusses the relationship between your revenue and your self-talk, the fundamental conversation behind very business professional's success.

What follows is a list of some of the harmful assumptions (in quotation marks) and negative self-talk (in italics) that untrained business professionals may be engaging in when approaching new business development:

"Anyone can do networking."

If the above is true, why do I find that my networking is so unproductive?

"I am good at what I do—referrals will naturally happen ."

If the above is true, why am I not receiving referrals?

"Anyone can develop a relationship."

If the above is true, why am I having difficulty developing productive business relationships?

4. "I'll just work really hard and give great service; clients will automatically seek me out."

Why aren't clients seeking me out?

Other Possible Negative Thoughts

I'm too good at what I do to be in a sales role.

Sales is easy.

Sales is sleazy and for hucksters.

And that's just a start.

As long as business or sales professionals allow any negative beliefs about new business development to take root and fester in their unconscious mind, they'll never reach their full revenue potential. In other words, *the effective creation of your revenue is directly tied to your thoughts.*

Positive, Powerful Thoughts = Increased Revenue

Thoughts to Review:

Do I need to review my thoughts to ensure that they are powerful and positive?

Will more positive thoughts have an impact on my revenue?

Do I want to change my self-talk?

SABOTEUR #3: THE "FEAR OF REJECTION" SALES SABOTEUR

Statement #3: "I embrace rejection in new business development" Never? Not often? Sometimes?

Not only do business professionals need to manage their daily activities along with their self-talk, they must also be fearless in their pursuit of their ideal customer, looking for the "no" in order that they may find the people who will say "yes." They need to be prepared for, and to welcome, a "no," as readily as they accept a "yes."

Some sales pundits suggest that you imagine yourself donning a uniform when you're prospecting so that when there is a poor fit with someone you can easily release any personal offense with the idea that, "It's the sight of my uniform that's triggering the poor response, not me." Business professionals need to protect themselves from perceiving business decisions as personal rejection.

Saboteur# 3, the "Fear of Rejection" Sales Saboteur, takes business professionals away from seeking the "no" that is so important to their qualifying process.

Wanting to belong to the pack is a primal need. All of us have this need—some of us more than others. What happens when this need is not fulfilled? How do you feel when your "belonging need" is not addressed? When, instead of feeling like you belong, you feel rejected because someone gave you a "no"? Well, the short answer is, not very good. And, certainly, you do not feel like taking on the world, as you search for your next new client. Why? Because *it* may happen again. Yes, you may risk *rejection*— that horrible feeling of not belonging. And yet, it is rejection that you must seek in your new business development process. It sounds strange, and it's true. You must be brave enough to seek out rejection. Rejection, in the new business development process, means that you become clear that a *suspect* is not a *prospect*. A *suspect is* someone who *might* be interested in your services; they are not necessarily a *prospect*, someone who *is* interested in, and needs, your services. If they are not a prospect, you move on, head high, to the next opportunity.

But not everyone can do that. There are some business professionals who have been burned by an earlier experience of rejection or perceived rejection by others, in childhood or more recently in their career. There is a deeper wound of some sort that does not let them get past the rejection process in new business development and move towards the creation of more sales. And then the wound festers . . . with more fears and more procrastination on the new business development front. Ultimately, the business professional may become frozen in their tracks, incapable of moving forward because of their fear of rejection. In order to break this trend, these fears need to be exposed— and expelled! Once this balance is achieved, the business professional can execute on their new business development activities. Expelling these fears means that there is **Good News Ahead:**

The Rejection goes both ways. The business professional must decide if their suspect/prospect is a good fit, too! *Hasn't everyone worked with a client who was a bad fit?*If you use referral marketing as your main new business development method, as discussed later in Chapter 9, you can teach your referral sources or partners about the ideal client that you wish to serve. They can do the searching and qualifying for you, *no rejection process required!*

Thoughts to Review:

- Are fears crippling my new business development growth?
- Do I have any fears of rejection that get in the way of my new business development activities?
- Am I ready to reach out to my network for referrals without fear of rejection?
- What tactics can I use to ensure that I don't take rejection at work personally, to remind myself that it's just business?

Saboteur #4:
The "Fears Tied to Revenue" Sales Saboteur

Statement #4: "Opportunities with new business development excite me" Never? Not often? Sometimes?

There are so many common self-limiting beliefs, or negative internal dialogues, about the sales process, that I have dedicated a special spot to the revelation of the "Fears Tied to Revenue" Sales Saboteur.

It is so empowering to think that you make your living, and your life, helping others by offering your services wrapped in your own unique blend of training, experience and personality. There is much to celebrate here, when you think of the lifestyle and income that can come with a "living by your wits" world. As you explore this endless horizon that being a professional service provider can unlock, however, you must also be aware of the newts and salamanders that can be lurking within your unconscious mind. They can have a serious, and sometimes fatal, impact on your ability to generate the income you deserve. How so? As discussed with Sales Saboteurs # 1–3, every negative thought about sales can have a negative effect on your revenue.

The spotlight is now on Sales Saboteur # 4, reminding you that every piece of self-doubt, or personal belief that does not serve you, can and *will* affect your performance on the new business development front. Self-limiting beliefs are held in everyone's unconscious. They are a well-known phenomenon to coaches and other professionals who facilitate the unleashing of these devils that hold all of us back from our greatness—and our happiness. How do these beliefs show themselves in your new business development

66

efforts? Here are a few examples of common self-limiting beliefs about new business development that I have witnessed or experienced myself:

• I can't talk to CEOs or senior people at prospective organizations. (Many reasons are given to rationalize this statement.)

• I can't pursue business with my ideal client because I don't deserve the income those conversations will create.

• I am not entitled to talk to a person with their resources—they are so much wealthier and more powerful than me!

• I am not strong enough in the required area of expertise (in spite of my many years of preparation within the specialty).

If you pile these fears onto the world's view of salespeople, you might get thoughts that sound like this:

• "I hate sales—I feel sleazy."

• "I don't like new business development. Can someone else do this?"

• "How can I be asked to bring in new clients? I worked hard at becoming a technical expert in my field so I would never have to be a sales rep."

• "I'm an introvert, I don't have the gift of the gab for sales."

The list goes on and on. Unfortunately.

Thoughts to Review:

• What are your self-limiting beliefs?

• Would one of your self-limiting patterns be around rejection?

• Are these beliefs holding you back from your success?

• Is it time to address the beliefs that affect your revenue?

Saboteur #5:
The "Scarcity" Sales Saboteur

Statement #5: "I see abundance everywhere" Never? Not often? Sometimes?

PMA or Positive Mental Attitude is another key asset in generating your own revenue. You must believe that you will succeed, have a clear goal of the revenue that you would like to attain each year, make adjustments when problems arise and celebrate when your success is realized. It might be surprising that an abundance mentality is an important addition to your revenue-building toolkit. But if you assume abundance, believe in your business and yourself, equip yourself with all of the right tools and training, some of which are outlined in Chapter 10, you will succeed.

Stay away from scarcity and all of its "little deaths." Saboteur #5, the "Scarcity" Sales Saboteur will always be in your way until you dismiss it.

What is a scarcity mindset? It's when the business professional's attitude is ungenerous toward him- or herself—and to the world about them. For example, business professionals with a scarcity mindset do not give out referrals, thinking that they are limiting their own pool of prosperity by doing so. A scarcity mindset is one of the most dangerous mindsets to have when developing new business and it puts a business professional in a position of taking, rather than sharing. In protecting their own interests, and not helping others, they ultimately let fear, instead of abundance, rule their hearts.

That prevents them from furthering their relationships with people and keeps them from achieving the goals they have set out to achieve and this severely limits a business professional's opportunities for referrals, the main method of developing new business for the majority of professional service providers.

Why would a scarcity mindset—an ungenerous, selfish attitude—have a negative effect on the referrals that a business professional would receive? Because a referral is a transfer of trust. Trust is not generated in a transactional environment where an individual is making sure that they get exactly what they give, and only give back accordingly. Trust is generated in an atmosphere of abundance.

If you want to develop new business for yourself, *give* a referral to a member of your network. (Of course, it would be wise to select the *right* member of your network and develop that relationship, executing with them on an excellent Booked Solid Referral Marketing Plan©. More to follow on this point in Chapter 8—Saboteur Prevention.)

What's more, a business professional's fear about their ability to grow their new business will certainly be misunderstood as something entirely different. Like desperation. *Desperation does not attract referral sources or partners—and definitely not clients.* It repels people and prospects. Keep away from a scarcity mindset. It will not serve you. Ever.

Thoughts to Review:

- Am I demonstrating a scarcity mindset to my network?
- Could that mindset be affecting my new business development?
- Do I want to do anything about my scarcity mindset?

SABOTEUR #6:
THE PROCRASTINATION SABOTEUR

Statement #6: "I always move forward when I need to" Never? Not often? Sometimes?

I often hear from business professionals that their business is cyclical. They say that there are peaks and valleys to their business. And yet, when we drill down to their sales funnel and the activity that led to their prospects and closed deals, it becomes clear that the business professional does not have a cyclical business, rather they have cyclical behaviour. That is, their activity, or lack thereof, generates the respective peak or valley three months later. They may work very hard on their new business development activity for three months, generate the appropriate revenue, and spend the next three months fulfilling their client's requirements, doing little or no business development. Then they conclude that they are in a cyclical valley. They are not aware that it is of their own making.

You can even out the peaks and valleys that you inadvertently create for yourself by consistently and frequently investing regular and considerable amounts of time and effort in your networking and referral-building activities. It then becomes clear that you can control your revenue and lifestyle quality by developing a daily routine designed to support the right new business development activities, which add regular social capital deposits to your network. This might sound difficult at first, but it will eventually feel much easier.

By embracing this critical point, through creating the Booked Solid Referral Marketing Plan© and, most importantly, executing on your plan, you will reach your revenue targets. While you may have managed your *negative self-talk and self-limiting beliefs and re-framed rejection, you will also need to watch out for Sales Saboteur # 6, the "Procrastination Saboteur." This Saboteur prevents you from acting on your plan and reaching your goals. It whispers in your ear that you have that all-important paperwork or some other pressing issue to address before you can go and out and build your client base. Consistent daily new business development activities that grow your network are always the most important part of your day. Always.*

Remember: Consistent activity = Consistent revenue

Procrastination gets in the way of reaching any goal, personal or business. When it comes to new business development, a habit of procrastination can be especially lethal, for two reasons.

The first reason is that when you procrastinate with new business development, it has a direct effect on your income. When your income is affected by your own behaviour, you have reason to be unhappy. That frustration can lead to other slippery slopes such as immobilization, self-blame and, ultimately, these emotions could lead to your exit from the business. That's not what you want!

New business development activities must be done on a daily basis and that leaves no room for procrastination! Here's the reality: if you set out and follow a daily routine of new business activities, you will have a steady growth line in your business development.

There is always room for investigating new and unexpected opportunities as they arise. As long as that occurs within a larger framework of consistent behaviour. Conversely, if you choose to procrastinate on your new business development activity plan, your new business results will directly and negatively reflect the energy that you have invested (or not).

It works well when there is a good plan in place and no procrastination. It is an unfortunate equation when the opposite is the case and the activity is inconsistent. Here are the energy numbers:

Daily, well-planned business development activities = Steady growth in actual business results

Inconsistent business development activity = Peaks and valleys in actual business results

Every business professional should take a close look at their monthly business results in light of their own new business development activities. They may observe that their current results are tied to a lot, or lack, of activity three to six months earlier.

If procrastination should rear its ugly head in your business, then the life-giving flow of new revenue will most surely be negatively affected. So, there can be no room for procrastination when new business development is at stake.

Thoughts to Review:

- Have I been procrastinating on new business development?
- Has my procrastination affected my income?
- What is my daily routine with new business development?
- Would The Booked Solid Referral Marketing Plan© help me to embrace a healthier daily new business development routine?

Saboteur #7:
The Lack of Resilience Saboteur

Statement #7: I bounce back easily when challenged. Never? Not often? Sometimes?

It is important to cultivate a mental toughness in new business development so you don't hurt yourself and your revenue. This quality allows you to bounce back from a tough question or a negative or difficult situation and it builds self-confidence.

At some point in your relationship, your client is going to challenge you.

If you remain calm and keep your ego and your emotions in check, you can focus rationally on finding the solution to the challenge. This will allow you to find a creative win/win solution that allows you and your client to move forward and close the deal together.

The "Lack of Resilience" Sales Saboteur prevents you from protecting yourself and encourages you to crumble in the inevitable face of adversity. This Saboteur wants you to cave in to the challenges of the moment and to give in to its mean spirit as it calls out your name.

Resilience has become a very popular word and we are often told that it is the most sought-after trait that employers seek in their prospective employees. It is also the most desirable trait that you can bring to your new business development efforts.

What does resilience look like in a new business development context?

Here are some thoughts:

1. You are not afraid to find out that there is no fit between you and your prospect.

2. You are tough enough to learn to lead the sales call.

3. You seek out the real truth about your closing opportunities with your prospects. You do not put "teddy bears" in your pipeline. Teddy bears are prospects who have a very low likelihood of closing for business. They are present in the pipeline merely to make the pipeline owner feel good by adding to the total numbers of prospects.

4. You are ready to put your prospect into "pain," asking well-placed questions that help them discover their real reason for seeking out your services. A resilient business professional always dares to discover if there really is a well-qualified opportunity.

They always find a way to make it happen:

The *resilient* business professional is unafraid to hear a "no" from a prospect. As a result, they get creative. They look at the global vision at the heart of their prospect's need and assess the small details that will make a difference to their results.

They come to really understand and embrace the client's challenges, and figure out a way to meet their need with their services. **They are determined to win the business.**

And so, if the business professional is not clear on the value of resilience, they might end up with the following results:

1.   They may blame the customer, their boss or anyone else they can find for their lack of momentum.
2.   They are likely to give up too early in the closing process.
3.   They are not likely to develop that right-sized solution for the prospect.
4.   They may not develop a winning mindset in sales.
5.   They may grow to dislike new business development.

There are many reasons why a business professional may not have the required amount of resilience to close business.

It boils down to a lack of certainty, a lack of clarity that sabotages the business professional, denying them the opportunity to reach their full potential.

In these situations, the Resilience Sales Saboteur moves into the gap to find a home, unfortunately.

Thoughts to Review:
- What is my level of resilience?
- What is my level of resilience with new business development?
- If I am not where I want to be, do I want to do anything about it?

SABOTEUR #8:
THE LACK OF SELF-ESTEEM SALES SABOTEUR

Statement #8: I feel good about myself.
Never? Not often? Sometimes?

Personal resilience can help you grow your business effectively by growing yourself. Another personal characteristic that is important for business growth is to maintain a healthy self-esteem.

By showing the world a constant positive face about you and your business, you lead your network and your prospects into conversations that will move your business forward and avoid as many problems as possible in the effort to succeed.

Happy, convincing business owners create solid and positive business results.

Take care of your self-esteem and your network will thank you with opportunities galore.

Saboteur # 8, the "Lack of Self-Esteem" Sales Saboteur, takes the business professional to a place where he or she is not offering up the positive world view that members of their network require before transferring valuable trust to create referrals.

Conviction Sells. It attracts all of the right energy for developing new clients and if the business professional in front of you demonstrates his or her belief in their ability to solve your problem wholeheartedly, you are more likely to refer someone to them or engage them yourself for their services. Aren't you?

If the business professional in front of you is talking about their bad day, their frustration with a client or the problem they had with parking, are you going to be interested in their business? Maybe, but likely *not*.

Bad news is easy. We can wallow in it, swim in it and make a real meal out of it. The "Lack of Self-Esteem" Saboteur would like us to do so. I encourage you to resist this Saboteur, and its temptation to focus on the negative side of life. When you own your own business, it is very important to maintain a healthy self-esteem and send out only positive messages to your network.

How does the business professional demonstrate their belief in their success? By maintaining a very positive energy around themselves and their business. Daily.

Self-esteem is about how you feel about yourself on any given day. Your positive energy about yourself helps your clients and your prospects have greater confidence in you. And it results in exponential business growth. Imagine how that would feel!

What's the relationship between how a business professional manages their self-esteem and their success in new business development? And, if it does have an impact on their new business development success, can they do something about harnessing and maximizing this asset? *Yes, you can manage and maximize your self-esteem. And it is very important to do so.*

Here's the key strategy: You need to respect this precious resource, your self-esteem, *and nurture it the same way that you would nurture your bank account.* With regular deposits. With an ongoing positive cash position. Some quick self-esteem nurturing tips include:

> • Identify what makes you happy. Passions? Reading? Sports? Your spouse? Your family? Friends? Make sure that your daily life is full of the activities that make you happy.
> • Choose your career/business accordingly.
> • Refer to and adopt all of Dr. Laura's "Body First" tips in Chapter 7 - The Antidotes to the Saboteurs.

Every business professional should have their own plan for the daily upkeep and development of their self-esteem.

Stay away from The "Lack of Self-Esteem" Saboteur. Make sure that you make those daily deposits in your own emotional bank account so you can enhance the enjoyment of your own life, and build your confidence and positive energy. It is one of the best new business development decisions you can make.

Thoughts to Review:

- Do I demonstrate conviction to my network?
- On a scale of 1 to 10, what is my daily self-esteem level?
- How can I boost my self-esteem?
- Do I have strategies for maintaining my self-esteem?
- If not, is my lack of strategies getting in my way?

SABOTEUR #9
THE MONEY SALES SABOTEUR

Statement #9: I enjoy my relationship with money. Never? Not often? Sometimes?

People who have a positive relationship with money, where they truly manage their money, are wealthy, indeed. And these people represent a small, very small, minority of the business professional population.

Most people have challenges with money, in one form or another. If a business professional has a relationship with money that has any fear, scarcity or anxiety attached to it, it will show in their revenue—and not in a good way. The "Money" Sales Saboteur has taken over their inner sanctum and the lizard brain is running their affairs.

Saboteur # 9, the "Money" Sales Saboteur, is a "stealth" Saboteur. It can hold quiet, deep power over the mindset of business professionals who want to succeed. A business professional may develop and execute positive, and very detailed, new business development habits, and not create the revenue of their dreams.

Somewhere, lurking deep in their unconscious mind is the "Money" Saboteur whispering odious phrases such as, "Rich people are not nice," "You do not deserve to be wealthy; you come from a poor family," or "You do not want to be too different from your peers." There are many more phrases that could be repeated by the "Money" Saboteur. It is an endlessly resourceful Saboteur.

"A mark, a yen, a buck or a pound, Money makes the world go round," is the quote from the movie *Cabaret* that comes to my mind when I think about our complicated relationships with money. And there are many other songs that speak of money and the emotions that we attach to this powerful force in our world. It has a kaleidoscope of different effects on our personal and professional relationships, and in the scope of achievements we are able to generate for ourselves and those we hold dear. It's important to pay attention to this giant, isn't it?

Money is the lifeblood of a business professional's practice or business. If money is flowing, the business is flourishing. If money is not flowing, the business and its owner can be deeply affected. It may even show on the outside to others.

Attracting new business becomes a challenge as the air of desperation and scarcity overrides the warmth and sense of abundance that so effectively encourages new clients to work with you. And a deadly cycle is created: The original challenge of disappointing new business results can create a mindset that leads to worsening results. And that's not the end of it — *at all.*

When a new client or prospect does finally arrive, the scarcity mindset can lead to the crafting of a bad deal, which sets the new relationship up for failure. For example, you may end up undercharging the client because you are desperate and do not see the value that you provide … and you leave a lot of money on the table as a result.

Or, you may craft a deal that is full of problems and does not serve you, and maybe not even the client. Desperation does not lead to creativity. It leads to bad decisions and poor client relationships.

The ugly reality for business professionals is that their attitude to money, as well as their family members' view of financial matters, is directly related to their business success.

If they have been told by family members that "money is the root of all evil," "money does not grow on trees," or, worse, there is no discussion of money at home, most business professionals who have not received any other kind of training about money will end up with some debilitating financial habits.

These attitudes may appear to be helpful when presented as frugality or respect for money.

At the same time, if $1,000 seems like a lot of money to you, you will be intimidated by larger amounts of money and might resist paying yourself according to your merit.

You could avoid your own success in order to continue to align yourself with your self-limiting beliefs. The lizard brain is powerful.

I repeat, *your mindset towards money is directly related to business success . . .* The equation looks like this: *Positive mindset +X mindset about money = $X of business revenue.*

Thoughts to Review:
- What are your current and ongoing beliefs about money?
- How do those thoughts affect your revenue and overall wealth?
- What do you want to do about your attitude toward money?

SABOTEUR #10:
The True Value of Your Services Sales Saboteur

Statement #10: I always ask for the true value of my services. Never? Not often? Sometimes?

The "Money" Saboteur manifests itself in many ugly ways. For business professionals, the "Money" Saboteur can appear at one of the most dangerous moments in their business life: when they present their fees for services to their clients. If the business professional is not resilient, has low self-esteem or is struggling with the "Money" Saboteur, it is very likely that they will not request the true value of their services.

When the client chooses to work with the business professional, and they can't believe how lucky they are to receive such high-quality service at such a low price, the business professional enters a hamster wheel of frustration. They are working hard for the client, delivering superior services, and not receiving appropriate compensation. This means that they must work harder to find new clients who will pay them the same low fees, creating the same resentment in the business professional that they felt with the original client from whom they did not request the right compensation.

Dangerous and undermining, this Saboteur invariably has a serious negative impact on a business professional's income, and it can be a very hard one to overcome. It is fitting, therefore, that this Saboteur be given its own category: the "True Value for Your Services" Sales Saboteur.

It may be surprising to learn that the impact of self-limiting beliefs and money fears reaches well past the confidence level of business professionals.

These *newts* and *salamanders,* these Saboteurs that already erode the confidence of business professionals, crawl right into their business offer to their clients.

So here's the bottom line: Not only do these self-limiting beliefs prevent the growth of new clients in the practice, they also minimize the revenue that the business or sales professional currently receives for their services. Scary, eh?

Here's how it works (or doesn't work!). Due to self-limiting beliefs and money fears, the business professional's overall level of self-confidence may be at a measly 4 out of 10. Most often, they take this precise level of confidence with them when evaluating the quality of services that they provide to their client. They may say to themselves, "The client will never pay x," or, "I am modest," or, "I am kind," or, "I don't want to be overcharging." While they are listening to this self-chatter, they are taking their pricing down and down to reflect the #4 confidence level with which they regard themselves.

That's right: How you price your services is directly related to your level of self-confidence — how you value yourself. Thus,

Level #4/10 Confidence = 40% of potential earnings
Let's move further down the spiral and ask the following question: Should you be using *your* evaluation of your services for the pricing of your services? Not at all.

The real money is made by evaluating the *true value that your client places on your services.* This thought leads to the very questions that business professionals often have not clearly answered in their own minds:

1.   What are the *real* problems that I solve for my specific, ideal client?
2.   Do I *really* understand both the emotional and business problems that I solve?
3.   Knowing or not knowing the answer to the first question, can I articulate the *real* value of my services to my client and to my referral network?

Thoughts to Review:

•   Is my level of confidence getting in the way of my true income potential?
•   Do I really understand my client's reasons for purchasing my services?
•   Have I ever identified any patterns or personal stories that have affected my confidence to ask for my true worth?
•   Have I addressed these patterns?

Conclusion to the Sales Saboteurs:

The Sales Saboteurs encompass a wide range of assumptions about new business development that do not serve business professionals well. Whether it is negative social attitudes toward the act of selling (Saboteurs #1 and #2) or the fears that arise from the resulting myths (Saboteurs #3 and #4), each of these beliefs must be reviewed and questioned for its relevance to your emerging new business development mindset.

Once you have addressed the big picture of what these myths represent in your world, you will want to look at any of the other Sales Saboteurs that prevent you from creating a new business development plan that requires three to four hours (includes lunch☺) of your time *every day*.

The payoff will be a much more powerful approach to your business, better sales results and stronger professional and personal relationships. Does that sound worthwhile?

You want to make sure that you stay away from the Sales Saboteurs that prevent you from executing on your plan. These Saboteurs include:

- lacking an attitude of abundance (Saboteur #5)
- procrastinating on daily activity plans (Saboteur #6)
- failing to maintain resilience (Saboteur #7) and
- failing to maintain a healthy level of self-esteem (Saboteur #8).

Finally, it is important that you closely review your attitudes toward money to find out if your financial mindset serves you well in business.

Start with the question, "Is my money serving me or am I serving my money?" (Saboteur #9). And then ask if you are obtaining the true value for your services (Saboteur #10).

Be alert to which of your answers are the same as they have always been, and which have changed over time. This will indicate that you have evolved, and help you determine what else needs to change in order to help you get the results you seek.

85

A final word: Overcome the Sales Saboteurs and adopt the recommended daily new business development behaviours and your life will never be the same again. Welcome to enjoyable new business development activities,

Phil, Francesca and Joe: What Are Their Sales Saboteurs (an X marks every applicable saboteur)?

Phil, the Beleaguered Business Owner of 20 Years

X Sales Saboteur #1: The "I Hate Selling" Sales Saboteur

X Sales Saboteur #2: The "Negative Self-Talk" Sales Saboteur

X Sales Saboteur #3: The "Fear of Rejection" Sales Saboteur

X Sales Saboteur #4: The "Fears Tied to Revenue" Sales Saboteur

X Sales Saboteur #5: The "Scarcity" Sales Saboteur

X Sales Saboteur #6: The "Procrastination" Sales Saboteur

X Sales Saboteur #7: The "Lack of Resilience" Sales Saboteur

X Sales Saboteur #8: The "Lack of Self-Esteem" Sales Saboteur

X Sales Saboteur #9: The "Money" Sales Saboteur

X Sales Saboteur #10: The "True Value of Services" Sales Saboteur

Phil's Sales Saboteurs had reached "takeover" level and they were running the show. After almost 20 years of being in the trenches, with unexamined prejudices about selling and sales people, Phil was plagued by all of the

Sales Saboteurs. In fact, he had scar tissue on many of his attitudes toward selling and he felt terrible. He was full of fears and procrastination habits, resulting in lack of self-esteem and personal resilience, all of which were compounded by money issues. He couldn't see a way out of the mess he was in and he needed a sound plan for moving forward.

It is not surprising that Phil wanted desperately to delegate sales to someone else, rather than do it himself. He had his work cut out for him.

Francesca, the Corporate Refugee (an X marks each Saboteur that affects her. Blank boxes are non-applicable):

X Sales Saboteur #1: The "I Hate Selling" Sales Saboteur

☐ Sales Saboteur #2: The "Negative Self-Talk" Sales Saboteur

X Sales Saboteur #3: The "Fear of Rejection" Sales Saboteur

X Sales Saboteur #4: The "Fears" Sales Saboteur

☐ Sales Saboteur #5: The "Scarcity" Sales Saboteur

☐ Sales Saboteur #6: The "Procrastination" Sales Saboteur

☐ Sales Saboteur #7: The "Lack of Resilience" Sales Saboteur

☐ Sales Saboteur #8: The "Lack of Self-Esteem" Sales Saboteur

X Sales Saboteur #9: The "Money" Sales Saboteur

X Sales Saboteur #10: The "True Value of Services" Sales Saboteur

Where did Francesca fit in this picture? She started her professional services firm with 5/10 Saboteurs in residence.

Saboteur #1, "I Hate Selling," was firmly nestled in Francesca's inner landscape and it led her to seek me out. Fortunately, her motivation to own her own business had not stopped her from giving in to her Saboteurs.

She was also a victim of Saboteur #3, the "Fear of Rejection" Saboteur, and Saboteur #4, the "Fears Tied to Revenue" Saboteur.

Since Francesca had embraced negative social attitudes toward the sales role, she had ingested traditional fears around rejection, selling activities, and not reaching out to prospects that were in executive roles.

Francesca had clear compartments in her mind as to "appropriate" conversations with her perceived "betters."

Finally, the omnipresent Saboteurs—Saboteur #9, the "Money" Saboteur, and Saboteur #10, the "True Value of Services" Saboteur — were present in Francesca's world.

Her perception of money in her business was tied to her own bank account and not to the perception of the value of the services she provided to her clients.

Unfortunately for Francesca, her own perception of the value of her services was considerably lower than the value that her clients put on her services.

Poor Francesca, it is very difficult to rise above a derisive attitude toward sales in any professional service environment.

Many professionals choose to excel down in the trenches of an area of technical expertise so that they *never* have to be in a sales role and it is safe to assume that the sales role is poorly regarded in most white-collar environments.

When a member of that environment makes the transition to a sales role, inevitably they will be infected by that attitude.

Joe, the Business Owner without Sleep (Each X marks a Saboteur that affects him)**:**

☐ Sales Saboteur #1: The "I Hate Selling" Sales Saboteur
X Sales Saboteur #2: The "I have Negative Self-Talk" Sales Saboteur
☐ Sales Saboteur #3: The "Fear of Rejection" Sales Saboteur
☐ Saboteur #4: The "Fears Tied to Revenue" Sales Saboteur
X Sales Saboteur #5: The "Scarcity" Sales Saboteur
☐ Sales Saboteur #6: The "Procrastination" Sales Saboteur
X Sales Saboteur #7: The "Lack of Resilience "Sales Saboteur
X Sales Saboteur #8: The "Lack of Self-Esteem" Sales Saboteur
X Sales Saboteur #9: The "Money" Sales Saboteur
X Sales Saboteur #10: The "True Value of Services" Sales Saboteur

Joe, our business professional who tossed and turned his night away, tracked at 6 out of 10 possible Saboteurs.

The Saboteurs were on their way to owning him, much like they had taken control of Phil.

Joe had embraced sales as a bona fide profession that added important value to the world and as a result he was not a victim of Saboteur #1.

However, he did have a lot of negative thoughts that rendered him a victim of Saboteur #2, "Negative Self-Talk about Business Development."

During his sleepless nights, Joe had courted Saboteur #5, the "Scarcity" Saboteur, thinking constantly about what was not happening and not nearly enough about what could happen…and learning about how he would make it so.

Partly due to his inability to sleep and partly due to his own mindset, Joe had become vulnerable to Saboteur #7, the "Lack of Resilience" Saboteur. He was not able to bounce back from any setbacks, and instead went right back to the "Scarcity" and "Negative Thoughts" Saboteurs.

As a result, he did not have the necessary focus and energy to maintain a positive mental attitude, which left him open to the overtures of Saboteur #8, the "Lack of Self-Esteem" Saboteur.

As is the case with many people, Joe was vulnerable to the "Money Saboteur."

He was being managed by his money, as per Saboteur #9, and he was driven by Saboteur #10 and not placing the appropriate value on his services.

Joe was tired, vulnerable and in a cocktail of trouble with the Saboteurs.

The Saboteurs and You:

Your Saboteur Self-Assessment answers will guide you to the specific areas that challenge you.

Have you read about every Saboteur that corresponds to a "1, 2 or 3" answer in your Saboteur Self-Assessment for Statements # 1-10?

What if you become aware of a Sales Saboteur that is not serving you, and it is not going away, in spite of your many efforts to rid yourself of it? *Perhaps, it is time to get some help?*

I believe that the best option is to consult a coach who specializes in new business development and who has both a track record of helping business professionals move forward and away from their fears, and a basket full of creative ideas that will help them keep options open for the future.

To avoid developing any Saboteurs, please take a look at the programs offered in Chapter 10, which include training and coaching in networking, referral-building and sales strategies.

And be prepared to invest your time in cultivating your new business development skills. It will take about two years, in total, to build your skill base.

Fortunately, you can take your courses one at a time, and that will help you develop your own referral marketing acumen.

You will need continuous ongoing reinforcement of your professional development after the first two years of skill-building until you are no longer required to create your own revenue.

A word of advice from one of my clients to his cronies crystallizes the reality and responsibility of business professionals acquiring new business development skills: "You can't take the elevator, you will have to take the stairs."

Thoughts to Review

- Do I have Sales Saboteurs?
- How many? Which ones?
- Do I want to do anything about them?
- Am I ready to develop my new business development skills? Now?
- Do I want to have fun creating my own revenue?

Chapter 6:
The Referral Saboteurs

"Help me," Mary said, "I can't do networking. I'm an introvert and I am paralyzed at events. I don't know what to do"

Mary was beautifully turned out in an elegant navy-blue suit with matching pumps. She had been in her own legal practice for more than five years, she was losing money daily and she was becoming frantic about her inability to create new clients for her practice.

She was considering closing down her posh office near her beautiful home in Greenwich, Connecticut, to take a gruelling job in the "City." She and her husband would be able to maintain the lifestyle to which they had become accustomed but Mary was terribly worried about the impact the change would have on the two wonderful children she had who were attending private schools.

I could see that Mary was in a lot of pain. I could also see the Referral Saboteurs chortle with glee as they quietly moved in and out of Mary's mind. They owned her completely.

"Mary," I said, "We have a lot to discuss. Let's start with some assumptions that you have made about yourself and networking . . ."

The mythology around networking is almost equivalent to that which surrounds the world of sales.

Mary had bought into much of it, including one of the most common and damaging beliefs: she had labelled herself an introvert as if it were a handicap for networking. We will be helping Mary with her perception of her introvert status with Referral Saboteur #22, a little later on in this section of the book. Here's a look at Referral marketing:

Referral marketing is a tried and true method of creating new business, and you might have heard a number of terms to describe this field, including:

1. Word of Mouth Marketing

2. Referral Marketing

3. High Touch© Marketing (vs. High Tech marketing)

4. Relationship Marketing

5. Local Marketing

This book uses the term "referral marketing" to describe the "marketing by referral" new business development method. A popular definition of referral marketing is that it is *"the systematic cultivation of business by referral."*

There are many myths about the field of referral marketing that bear investigation. The book, *Truth or Delusion: Myths about Networking*, counts 49 myths about networking, the key activity that leads to creating relationships and referrals. It was written by Dr. Ivan Misner, the founder of BNI, the world's largest networking group, and Mike Macedonio, President of the Referral Institute.

Forty-nine myths is a lot of myths. Who teaches us about networking anyway? Our parents. Or colleagues who know as little as we do. Or other helpful folks . . . . And their education in strategic networking comes from . . . ?

Given the lack of knowledge on this topic, you can imagine that the Saboteurs have a rich field to plow when it comes to networking and the fruits of these efforts...referrals.

These Saboteurs, let's christen them the Referral Saboteurs, can easily pounce upon an unsuspecting business professional.

For this is a very personal world, a world that is built upon people helping one another, leveraging their social capital and transferring their trust.

It's enough to send the vulnerable business professional back to the schoolyard.

Memories of *"The kids won't play with me, no one likes me,"* or *"I didn't make the team"* come to mind.

Well, come to think of it, the negative thoughts could have started there, right in the schoolyard. And they have been extended ever since. One sabotaging thought at a time.

The Referral Saboteurs and You

As I mentioned in Chapter 5, each statement in the Saboteur Self-Assessment has been organized to match its respective Saboteur.

If you have answered any of the Referral Saboteur Statements (#11 to #21),with a number between "1"and "3" ("never" to "sometimes"), you might want to look for more details about that Saboteur in this section.

For example, if you answered Statement #11, "I enjoy networking," with 1 "never," 2 "not often" or 3 "sometimes," you may want to read more about Saboteur #11, The "I Hate Networking" Referral Saboteur.

If you answered Statement #15, "I enjoy walking into a roomful of people," with 1 "never," 2 " not often" or 3 "sometimes," you may want to read more about Saboteur #15, the "Roomful of People" Referral Saboteur.

If you answered Statement #21, "I work with my ideal client," with 1 "never," 2 "not often" or 3 "sometimes," you may want to read more about Saboteur #21, The "I Refuse to Identify My Ideal Client" Referral Saboteur.

If you answered 4 "often" or 5 "always" to any of the #11 – #22 Referral Saboteur questions, you can congratulate yourself on resisting the Referral Saboteurs that correspond to the statement number.

At the same time, you may still want to learn more about that Referral Saboteur to make sure that you will recognize it when it presents itself to you, or a member of your network, in the future.

Once you are rid of the Referral Saboteurs, you will undoubtedly enjoy networking more—at events or face-to-face with members of your "Big 10" network, the Referral "A" team that trained referral marketers develop for themselves.

The Saboteurs in this list represent the top 12 Referral Saboteurs that I have observed during my years of coaching and training budding referral marketers — to recap this list, they are:

11.   I Hate Networking.
12.   No One Is Going to Refer Me.
13.   I Can't Refer Other People.
14.   Networking Does Not Work.
15.   I'm Not Comfortable Walking into a Room Full of People I Don't Know.
16.   I Don't Like Meeting New People.
17.   I Don't Like Small Talk.
18.   I Am Afraid to Give a Bad Referral.
19.   I Am Afraid to Receive a Bad Referral.
20.   I Am Not Organized (Electronically or Otherwise) to Follow Up on Referrals or Networking Opportunities.
21.   I Refuse to Define My Ideal Client.
22.   I Don't Have the Personality for Networking.

So, what is your Referral Saboteur? Let's identify them all. The more, the merrier! They hate the light . . .

Thoughts to Review:

• Do any Saboteurs on the Top 12 Referral Saboteurs list resonate with me?
• Do I have a Referral Saboteur to add to the list?
• Do I want to shine a light on any particular Referral Saboteur?
• Do I want to rid my life of a Referral Saboteur?

SABOTEUR #11
THE "I HATE NETWORKING" REFERRAL SABOTEUR

Statement #11: I enjoy networking. Never? Not often? Sometimes?

A Referral Saboteur is a negative thought that erodes the confidence of the business professional, affecting his or her ability to give or receive a referral.

Since most business professionals generate their new business through referrals, it is a serious matter when a Saboteur visits the unconscious mind of their unsuspecting owner and prevents them from moving forward and attending networking events.

The "I Hate Networking" Referral Saboteur:

"I Hate Networking" is the poster child of Referral Saboteurs. It is such a lethal negative thought that it has earned the top spot on the Referral Saboteur list.

It is a counterproductive thought because . . . *Without networking, there can be no referrals.*

One important way to shed light on this Saboteur is to define the term "networking." Networking happens when there is more than one person in a room. In other words, at least two people must be talking to one another in the same room for networking to occur and results to accrue.

Yes, that's right. It's a powerful thought, isn't it? Only two people. I find many of my clients take comfort from this point. They are not as intimidated by the thought of networking when they learn that when two people communicate with one another, they are networking.

And they always have the opportunity to deepen their relationship and create referrals for one another down the road.

For it is the content of that conversation, or of past conversations, that determines the possibility and quality of referrals that the relationship produces.

Two or more people who get together anywhere to network have the unique opportunity to learn more about one another. And to create trust. *Without trust, there can be no referrals. A referral is a transfer of trust.*

So here's the deal, el Saboteur: Networking can happen anywhere two or more people meet and create a new relationship.

Networking does not *only* happen at big, flashy events that can exponentially raise the anxiety levels of vulnerable business professionals, and giving you, Your Saboteurship, increased access to the soft underbelly of their unconscious mind.

Networking is not so much about the event. The event is merely the platform for the real story: *The real story is about the creation of new relationships. And the opportunity to grow trust between two people.*

Once that trust is established, and only when the trust is established, deep knowledge of one another's business will lead to more and better referrals.

Trust + Business Knowledge + Conviction = Great Referrals

Quality over quantity, every time.

So, connections are made at all events, large or small. It is the meaningful relationships, brimming with trust that will create referrals.

Thoughts to Review:

- Do I have relationships brimming with trust?
- Do I know how to leverage those relationships for referrals?
- Do I let a Saboteur in when I attend networking events?
- Do I want to learn more about networking and referral-building to create referrals?

SABOTEUR #12
THE "NO ONE WILL GIVE ME A REFERRAL!" REFERRAL SABOTEUR

Statement #12: "I think that people will give me a referral." Never? Often? Sometimes?

*One of the most common objections that I hear about referral marketing is that "I do not see why anyone would give **me** a referral."*

When a business professional is new to their own brand, they often have reservations about their experience and the services that they offer.

The "No One Will Give Me a Referral" Referral Saboteur must be addressed as soon as possible, after it arises.

There are a number of possible layers to the "No One Will Give Me a Referral" Referral Saboteur. Each layer attracts more Saboteurs:

1. No one will give me a referral because the world is not a generous place. (Scarcity Saboteur)

2. No one will give me a referral because the world is not generous to me. (Scarcity + Personal Saboteur)

3. No one will give me a referral because no one likes me. (Scarcity + Personal Saboteur + Self-Esteem Saboteur)

4. No one will give me a referral because

_____

(Fill in the blank.)

There might be some other ways to look at the "No One Will Give Me a Referral" statement:

1. No one will give a referral because I don't ask for referrals.

2. No one will give me a referral because I do not give referrals.

3. No one will give me a referral because I do not define clearly who I would like to meet, my ideal client.

4. No one will give me a referral because I do not give them any direction as to the specific size, type and specialty of the individual or organization with whom I would like to do business. My message implies that I will do business with anyone. (*This means that you will end up doing business with no one.)

5. No one will give me a referral because I have not identified the specific values that I would like to see in my client. My message does not include a picture of the kind of person with whom I would like to do business, including their education, their background, their interests, their beliefs. For example, "My ideal client is a professional service provider who is a lifelong learner and wants to grow their business by growing themselves. They appreciate and take advice, and are coachable and motivated to take their business to the next level."

Hmmm, so maybe the Saboteurs are not only taking the business professional to the wrong places but are also clouding the fact that there is help to be found through learning? Learning about how to create referrals? All the more reason to bring in the light with referral marketing knowledge and skills.

Thoughts to Review:

- Do I have a "No One Will Give Me a Referral" Saboteur in my thoughts?
- Do I have any other Referral Saboteurs?
- Do I want to receive more referrals?
- Do I want to learn more about how to create referrals?

SABOTEUR #13
THE "I CAN'T REFER OTHER PEOPLE" REFERRAL SABOTEUR

Statement #13: I refer other people. Never? Not often? Sometimes?

A concern that presents itself to business professionals who are starting to implement referral marketing principles is that they do not see how they can refer other people.

There are building blocks to creating a referral that they have yet to learn. Once you have learned and implemented the construction of these building blocks, and made space for any creative new ideas that might add value to your plan, this Referral Saboteur fades away.

You learn how to provide referrals to your network and, ultimately, to develop a convincing track record of referral marketing. You become confident in your ability to create a referral and want to develop referrals for the right people in your network.

A Referral Saboteur of any kind is defined as a negative thought or layers of negative thoughts that prevent business professionals from networking to build the revenue that they deserve.

One of the most common yet damaging Referral Saboteurs is "I Can't Refer Other People." This particular Referral Saboteur can be quite dangerous, because it creates a knot of Saboteur threads, cascading with all sorts of conflicting thoughts.

Here is the list of threads (and their antidotes) that might be found, in whole or in part, in the thinking of the business professional who states that he or she "cannot give a referral."

Thread #1: He/She doesn't know how to refer people.

Antidote Learning to create a good referral requires a surprising number of skills. It is no small matter and it has huge implications. As Phil learned earlier in the book, you need to acquire three major skill sets: networking, referral-building and preparing and executing on the sales process, all of which must be grounded in the right mindset, wrapped into a solid referral marketing plan. Acquiring the appropriate mindset and skill sets to create an excellent referral makes a real difference to your confidence and comfort level. And it does not stop there. You need to maintain the mindset and skills. Accountability is critical in the referral world. Please refer to Chapter 10 for more help.

Thread #2   He/She doesn't know enough about others to refer them.

Antidote Business professionals would serve themselves and members of their network well by learning more about one another's businesses. A good referral marketing plan supports the key 1:1 activity of meeting regularly with selected members of one's network. Once trust has been established the next step in creating a referral is to learn more about one another's business. It's the key to building the credibility that leads to a solid referral.

Thread #3   He/She may not be disposed to create business via leveraging relationships by referral.

Antidote It is important to note that some people are not inclined to leverage their personal and professional relationships for business. The budding referral marketer needs to be able to identify these individuals, as mutually beneficial referrals are unlikely to result. Some people are simply transactional in their approach. They are not relationship-oriented and not truly interested in the power or the results of the referral-creation process. You can look for signs of this type of individual by gauging their interest in other people's businesses when you meet them at networking events or during your 1:1 sessions. If they are not the "sharing" or "giving" type, they are not going to want to participate in a referral relationship. It's just not their element. The good news? The more you build your own referral marketing skill sets, the more likely you will be able to recognize who is wired for the referral world. And, frankly, I suggest that you choose members of your network accordingly. Does that sound like a good idea?

Thread #4   He/She *may not trust* members of their network and are not able to transfer the trust that is fundamental to creating a referral.

Antidote: Deeper work is required here. I am sorry to say that if trust is not in the lexicon of a potential member of your referral network, you are well advised to run, not walk, away from this relationship, at least as it pertains to referrals. These individuals may be important to you in other ways, but not as a source of referrals. The basic trust is not there.

The best ways to eradicate the "I Can't Refer Other People" Referral Saboteur from your professional practice are as follows:

1. Build your referral marketing skill sets. There are a total of 160 referral marketing strategies available to you, and only 40 of them are needed to create an effective referral marketing plan for yourself and your business. Create the plan and make sure that you are fully accountable. Please refer to Chapter 10 for details on assistance with developing your plan.

2. Develop a referral-building mindset. Clear out all Saboteurs, keep them out, let in abundance and give, give, give . . .

3. And give to the right people. Learn how to identify the ones you can trust, who know and like your business and who are your raving fans.

In summary, referral marketing is the *uncommon application of common practices.*

Incorporate those common practices daily into your business and you will be well on your way to building, and giving, referrals. And to waving a not-so-fond farewell to this Referral Saboteur.

Thoughts to Review:
- Do I feel that I can't refer other people?
- Do I need to build my referral-building skill sets?
- Do I have a crystal-clear giving mindset, teeming in abundance?
- Do I need to do some pruning with my network and focus on the right people?

SABOTEUR #14
THE "NETWORKING DOESN'T WORK" REFERRAL SABOTEUR

Statement #14: I believe that networking works. Never? Not Often? Sometimes?

The idea of creating business opportunities by leveraging their personal network does not sound entirely appealing to all business professionals. For this reason, it is important for you to establish whether referral marketing is a method that feels right for you.

If there is a question about how effective networking looks to be as a bona fide method of developing new business, you will be vulnerable to a lot of second-guessing, generated by your own thoughts. And, with these second guesses come the first line of the Saboteurs.

Saboteurs are very fond of any openings in the unconscious mind of the business professional. Any thought that brings on self-doubt, lack of confidence or erosion of a solid approach to self is easy pickings for the Saboteur. For a Saboteur preys upon your conviction, diminishing your ability to be at your best.

One very common Referral Saboteur is the belief that "Networking does not work." The business professional may not realize that they hold this belief within their unconscious mind. And they may retain this belief for any number of reasons:

1. ***They may not like cold calling yet they have adopted the assumptions behind cold calling.*** Assumptions such as, "It's a numbers game; the more people you talk to *(regardless of the depth that you are developing in the relationship)*, the more business you'll get." Then there's, "If you have the intestinal fortitude to pick up that 500 lb. phone you'll bulldoze the way to success."

2. ***The business professional may intellectually embrace the idea that networking works.*** They may actually *believe* something very different. Again, easy pickings for the Referral Saboteurs.

3. ***A relational mindset is required for networking success.*** In other words, the business professional must have a strong personal value about the importance of relationships in business. A transactional attitude toward relationships that is continually focused on the balance of power will not achieve all the results that business by referral promises. Until a relationship-oriented mindset is developed, a business professional, who is transactional in their approach will not be well-suited for the referral world.

4. ***They have not had a lot of personal success with networking.*** And this result could be for a lot of reasons. If you are assuming failure as a result, for example, you will definitely get it.

5. ***The business professional has not noticed that any business has come from networking.*** Business by referral can be murky and complex. A conversation three years ago could have resulted in a new referral today.

And there are many more examples of the reasons for the "Networking Does Not Work" Saboteur to flourish in the minds of business professionals.

Of course, this entire book assumes that networking does work. What is the proof? Well, some of the proof comes from experience. Think about how new clients have come to your practice or business. Could you draw a mind-map of the relationships that brought them into your fold? What percentage of your new business has come by referral?

And even in this murky world of referrals, there is the solid statistic that referrals have a 34 per cent closing rate. Not bad compared to the 1 per cent closing rate offered by cold calling. Networking *does* work. And millions of business professionals have learned this through their own experience.

And so what is the antidote to "Networking Does Not Work?" To start, find out the reasons for this assumption. Discussions with your Booked Solid referral marketing coach will quickly isolate the Saboteurs that created these thoughts. Then it is important to drill down to find out how these beliefs came to be. And send the Referral Saboteurs out to the cold, where they belong.

Thoughts to Review:
- Do I believe that networking works?
- Can I track where my new business comes from?
- Do I want to do more business by referral?
- Do I want to learn more about doing business by referral so I can keep the Saboteurs away?

SABOTEUR #15 – THE "ROOM FULL OF PEOPLE I DON'T KNOW" REFERRAL SABOTEUR

Statement #15: I am always comfortable walking into a room full of people. Never? Not often? Sometimes?

*Is it really a Referral Saboteur or is it just part of human nature to be reluctant to walk into a room full of people we don't know? Well, if you are **not** attending networking events at all due to the persistent presence of this thought, then, yes, most certainly, it is a Referral Saboteur. Without a regular, formalized and organized networking or referral marketing plan that leaves room for pleasant surprises, a business professional who is responsible for generating their own revenue is not able to continue to create a fresh supply of valuable contacts for themselves and for members of their network.*

Since formal networking (and informal networking as well) is vital to your business health, what do you do when you're not so ready to boldly enter a room full of strangers?

At this point, it is important to acknowledge that everyone has days when they do not feel like entering a room full of people, brimming with risks and the challenge of where to start. Even off-the-charts Influencers-Promoters (the fast-paced, people-friendly behaviour style), like me, have moments like these. And they can happen for any number of reasons: perhaps the business professional is exhausted or vulnerable or, just maybe, because his or her soul hurts that day. So what are the antidotes for the challenging times when you must attend a networking event even though you are not feeling so tickety-boo? Here are a few ideas:

1.   Call up one of the eight to ten treasured members of your network and ask them to come with you to the event. (You don't have network members with whom you can do this? Is it time to be thinking about creating a network that will support you in this way?)

2.   Approach a staff member of the host organization and identify the connections that you would like to make.

3.   Approach a member of your network at the event and ask for their help with connecting.

4.   Take a moment for yourself to acknowledge the fatigue, vulnerability or hurt in your soul. If you are tender with yourself for a few minutes, you will be surprised at your readiness to move forward.

5.   If your reluctance to work the room continues, seek out networking and referral marketing coaching and training. Chapter 10 will provide you with some ideas.

Any one of these five strategies will send those Referral Saboteurs back where they belong: **NOWHERE!**

Thoughts to Review:

•   Do I have eight to ten treasured members of my network who know the needs that I address and the solutions that I provide?

•   Could I turn to any one of them for help with Referral Saboteur #15?

•   Do I need assistance with networking and referral marketing strategies to create the informed eight- to ten-person network that I require to grow my business?

•   Do I want to create The Booked Solid Referral Marketing Plan© to ensure that Referral Saboteurs never have their way with me?

SABOTEUR #16 – THE "I DON'T LIKE MEETING NEW PEOPLE" REFERRAL SABOTEUR

Statement #16: I like meeting new people. Never? Not often? Sometimes?

The phrase "I don't like meeting new people" is definitely worthy of the Referral Saboteur designation.

Not liking or wanting to meet new people is a negative thought that seriously limits the growth of your network.

It is undoubtedly a Referral Saboteur. In a formal networking environment, there are two objectives for networking:

1. To meet new people

2. To re-connect with current members of your network, briefly, while meeting new people

So, either way, meeting new people is a core reason for the entire networking endeavour.

It may or may not surprise you to hear that I have heard many business professionals say that they do not like meeting new people.

I have also heard some business professionals confess that they are frightened of meeting new people.

Why would anyone not like or even be frightened of meeting new people? Let me count the ways:

1. As discussed earlier, where have most business professionals received their training on networking? *From their parents. And, maybe, colleagues and supervisors. All of whom are likely to be unschooled in the referral marketing world.* If you've had no real training on how to meet people, you can be at a disadvantage. Some business professionals may dislike meeting new people as a result.

2. When a business professional is not trained properly for networking, or for any other new client development activity, s/he is often put into a position of uncertainty. This lack of knowledge creates insecurity and affects self-confidence. An already vulnerable business professional, who does not really see the "big picture" when it comes to networking, can be exposed to numerous individual situations that can make him/her very uncomfortable. The net result? "I don't like networking," or, "I don't like meeting new people."

3. A person may have had a series of negative experiences with meeting new people in their childhood. If their parents moved around a lot or the business professional had some childhood trauma with new kids at school, s/he can develop a lot of fears about new people.

4. Unprocessed fears can grow to be very big Personal or Referral Saboteurs. Whether it is because of the above-mentioned childhood traumas or from a more recent malingering sales trauma, a business professional can grow to dislike meeting new people.

5. There can be other explanations for not liking to meet new people. Ultimately, these reasons fit into the categories here: lack of training, lack of preparation, unprocessed fears, or all of the above.

113

What are the Referral antidotes to these challenges outlined on the previous page?

1.   Learn more, and more, much more, about networking. You will never regret your investment in a high-quality, strategic training program on networking/referral-building. It also helps for business professionals to learn together.

2.   If you think that you might have the "I Don't Like Meeting New People" Referral Saboteur in your mindset, please do seek out the help of a Booked Solid referral marketing coach.

Once you have sent your Referral Saboteur packing, you will feel so much more confident about networking, relationships and, of course, meeting new people.

And, best of all, the "I Don't Like Meeting New People" Referral Saboteur will be out of your thoughts— and out of your life.

Thoughts to Review:

• Do I have this Referral Saboteur embedded in my thoughts?
• Do I need training in networking and referral-building?
• Do I want to recommend networking/referral-building to my team?
• Do I want to seek out a referral coach to address my Referral Saboteurs?

SABOTEUR #17 – THE "I DON'T LIKE SMALL TALK" REFERRAL SABOTEUR

Statement #17: I like small talk. Never? Not often? Sometimes?

The term "small talk" is a lot bigger than this phrase suggests. And not wanting to participate in this so-called idle conversation is a common objection for not wanting to network, the lifeblood activity for creating referrals. This referral tip drills down on the topic of small talk and why it is so important to the global project of building an effective network, one that provides ongoing referrals for your business or practice. Before we examine this Referral Saboteur more closely, let's define the term "small talk." Here's what Wikipedia has to say:

"Small talk is an informal type of discourse that does not cover any functional topics of conversation or any transactions that need to be addressed. [1]" (Source: https://en.wikipedia.org/wiki/Small_talk)

From our experience with the Referral Saboteurs and business professionals, we can see the seeds for the *trouble with small talk* in this phrase. We know that many business professionals are much more comfortable when there is a focus or direction to any activity, especially when the activity involves people.

And the Wizards of Wikipedia have more to say about small talk (is it such a *small* subject?):

"The ability to conduct small talk is a social skill; hence, small talk is some type of social communication. Early publications assume networked work positions as suitable for social communication.[3] . . . Newer habits

115

make use of social media as an instrument for small talk. [4]*" (ibid)*

You can see the Referral Saboteurs smirking in the background, waiting to pounce on their prey. A social skill? Newer habits? Social media? Rubbing their hands with glee, the Referral Saboteurs have found yet another vulnerable area where they can create further havoc in the minds of business professionals. They chortle, "Small talk can be made into a challenge, face-to-face *and* online!"

Social scientists help with our understanding of the dynamics of small talk, and with finding solutions to overcome our aversion to it, with the following comment:

"In spite of seeming to have little useful purpose, small talk is a bonding ritual and a strategy for managing interpersonal distance .[5]

It serves many functions in helping to define the relationships between friends, work colleagues, and new acquaintances. In particular, it helps new acquaintances to explore and categorize each other's social position[6]

Small talk is closely related to the need for people to maintain positive face (dignity, prestige) to feel approved of by those who are listening to them. It lubricates social interactions in a very flexible way." (ibid)

And so the social scientists confirm that there is much more to the "Small Talk" Referral Saboteur than meets the eye.

Imagine the Saboteur-prone business professional managing all of these elements of small talk, without a framework, training or strategies . . .

The real role of small talk in human interaction is to:

1.   "Lubricate" social interactions

2. Establish social status.
3. Function as a "bonding ritual."
4. Function as a communication strategy.
5. Demonstrate social skill.

Small talk — not so small. No wonder it's entertained the Referral Saboteurs so readily.

Add an intellectual and emotional framework, training, coaching and strategies and the Referral Saboteurs will be sent packing. And good riddance to this Referral Saboteur!

Thoughts to Review:

*   Do I acknowledge the importance of small talk in building my business, or do I dismiss it out of hand as superficial and unnecessary?"
*   Is a Referral Saboteur on small talk embedded in my thoughts?
*   Do I need a framework to help me with small talk?
*   Do I want training or more strategies to help me be more effective with small talk?
*   Do I want to seek out a referral coach to address this Referral Saboteur?

SABOTEUR #18 – THE "I'M AFRAID TO GIVE A BAD REFERRAL" REFERRAL SABOTEUR

Statement #18: I know what to do if I give a bad referral. Never? Not often? Sometimes?

The fear of giving a bad referral is a surprisingly common Referral Saboteur. And, like all Referral Saboteurs, this fear can prevent talented business professionals from reaching their full revenue potential. At this point, it is important to dig deeper into the topic of bad referrals.

How do bad referrals happen? Why do they happen?

A bad referral happens when the recipient of the referral, the vendor, is presented with a prospect who has not been qualified properly by the person giving the referral (the referral source).

As a result, the prospect is uninterested, unwelcoming or, worse, seems annoyed by the approach of the prospective vendor.

This doesn't sound like an enviable position for anyone, does it? And it feels horrible for the vendor. This is definitely not what a referral is about.

So who is responsible for the quality of the referral? The person who generates the referral. The referral source.

In effect, the referral source is transferring their trust to the recipient of the referral, the vendor. And, with this sacred transfer, a referral is born.

It is, therefore, the role of the referral source to qualify the prospect for the referral recipient or vendor. Some referral marketing pundits like to use the expression, "It's all my fault" to highlight the responsibility equation. It may seem a little nasty. And it's true.

Imagine what would happen if every referral generator took full responsibility for the referrals that they gave? The number of bad referrals would go way down.

And how do you qualify your network members in order to create a high quality referral for another member of your network? By one dedicated act. By using your two biggest assets. *Your ears, of course! By listening.* Yes, and listening *very deeply* so you can discover the following key characteristics of the ideal client of the referral recipient:

1. Type of organization (Business, Government, Professional Service Provider)

2. Size of organization (Yearly Revenue, Number of Employees)

3. Level in organization (Owner, V.P., Manager, Service)

4. Location(s)

5. Age and gender of organization leader

6. Behaviour style of leader (People like to deal with people who are like them)

7. Organizational Values regarding the service provided
8. Personal values that the business professional is seeking in their ideal client

9. Level of motivation of buyer

10. Budget commitment level

And much more . . .

Typically, the recipient of the referral, the vendor, does not have these 10 characteristics tripping off their tongue.

You, the potential referral source, should expect to help your network members with articulating these characteristics, to help them create the message that empowers you to create great referrals for them.

Herein lies the need to *listen deeply* . . . and carefully. To assist the referral recipient with helping themselves . . . by painting the picture of their ideal client.

With this quality of conversation, the referral source will never be prey to the "I Don't Want to Give a Bad Referral" Referral Saboteur.

Thoughts to Review:

- Do I worry about giving a bad referral?
- Do I need to listen more deeply for referral opportunities?
- Do I know 10 characteristics of my ideal client? Or of the ideal client of selected members of my network?
- Do I require coaching or training on my message?

SABOTEUR #19 – THE "I'M AFRAID TO RECEIVE A BAD REFERRAL" REFERRAL SABOTEUR

Statement #19: I know what to do if I receive a bad referral. Never? Not often? Sometimes?

The flip side of Referral Saboteur #18, "I'm Afraid to Give a Bad Referral," is Referral Saboteur #19, "I'm Afraid to Receive a Bad Referral." What do you do with a bad referral, if anything? The answer is not to "do nothing." To do nothing is to do "something". . . at your own peril.

An untrained networker who receives a bad referral, and does nothing about it, can be providing rich ground for developing a Referral Saboteur. This untutored networker can be saying to themselves, "Why should I try to grow my business by referral if I risk damaging the precious few relationships that I have?"

So what about this Referral Saboteur? How does the business professional tame this particular Referral Saboteur? Well, what *do* you do when you receive a bad referral? Here is the definition of a bad referral from the previous Referral Saboteur #18:

> "A bad referral happens when the recipient of the referral is presented with a prospect who is not qualified properly by the referral giver, also known as the referral source. As a result, the prospect is uninterested, unwelcoming or, worse, annoyed by the approach of the referral recipient, the prospective vendor."

The truth is that if you have received a bad referral from a colleague, then *you* are the one who is responsible

121

for setting the record straight. As established previously, the referral source is responsible for the success of the referral. It is important to go back to your referral source to discuss the misunderstanding that created the bad referral.

Here are five actions you might want to consider if you're on the receiving end of a bad referral and you're the unfortunate "prospect-chastened" business professional:

　　　1.　　Approach the giver of the bad referral, your referral source, and request a face-to-face meeting. Nothing less, please. You are embarking on a courageous conversation and you need to give your referral source the full benefit of your caring and generous body language.

　　　2.　　Before the meeting, be sure to review what you have been saying about your business or practice and how much of this message might have been received improperly by your referral sources, including the generator of the bad referral. You might need a few hours of coaching or training to de-clutter your message so you can avoid this problem in future. As a result of this message "house-cleaning," you can answer succinctly and clearly the five questions that all referral sources need to know about you, including who your ideal client is. And you will feel so much more confident.

　　　3.　　When you meet your referral source, thank them for the referral and tell them what happened when you approached the prospect. If you feel that the referral source had not been clear on your message, this is your chance to clarify the message with them.

4.   And, conversely, you will want to find out all about their ideal client introduction. As noted earlier, please don't be surprised if they have trouble articulating the characteristics of their ideal client. Most business professionals cannot identify the necessary specific traits of their ideal client.

5.   Make sure that you keep connected with the referral-giver and try to give them a referral as soon as possible.

Now you can see how bad referrals happen:

Bad information = Bad referrals

Does it make a difference to know that there are actions that you can take in the event of a bad referral? Oh, yes. These strategies arm you with precious knowledge that helps you to feel more in control of all of your future referral-building endeavours.

Input from your meeting with your referral source, and maybe some coaching on your message and your referral-building skills, will help you be able to look this Referral Saboteur in the eye and say, "Be off, Saboteur, be off!"

Thoughts to Review:
- Have I ever received a bad referral?
- Do I know the real reason behind a bad referral?
- Do I have a message that supports a good referral?
- Do I have a few Referral Saboteurs lurking in the corridors of my mind?
- Do I want them to "BE OFF?!"

SABOTEUR #20 – THE "I AM NOT ORGANIZED FOR FOLLOW-UP" REFERRAL SABOTEUR

Statement #20: I am adequately organized to follow up. Never? Not often? Sometimes?

This section addresses a Saboteur very like the one that we encountered in the Sales Saboteur section, the Procrastination Saboteur. When it comes to referrals, this one is all about finding reasons for not going to networking events and, by extension, for not following up. Referral Saboteur #20 boils down to this: "I don't have a follow-up system so networking will not work for me. Why bother networking?"

There are a few key points to consider about the "I Am Not Organized to Follow Up on Referrals or Networking Opportunities" Referral Saboteur. Each of these considerations is followed by comments and proposed antidotes:

1. As you know from your own experience, most networkers don't follow up after an event. Some studies point to the fact that more than 90 per cent of networkers do not follow up after networking events.

Antidote: Most of mankind would not be networking if they listened to Referral Saboteur #20. Let's see if you can do better with a post-networking follow-up routine.

2. Once a follow-up routine is embraced, the window for this activity after a networking event used to be 72 hours, but times have changed. I now suggest that 24 hours, preferably much less, is the

maximum period of time to give yourself for follow-up after a networking event. Life moves quickly and your new connection has moved on to other new connections and networking events. And life events happen, as well, and your new contacts become distracted.

Antidote: If you have not followed up for over a week, it will be difficult to keep yourself top of mind with your new connection. If you have a pile of cards and have not followed up with the card owners for more than six months, you might want to forgive yourself, let go of your guilt and let go of the cards. They are now stale-dated for you and your connections.

3. It is easy to become overwhelmed and discouraged with your follow-up record if you come back from every event with a stack of business cards and you never get around to doing anything with them. A lot of networkers think that gaining a lot of business cards is the main goal for attending a networking event.

Antidote: You might want to consider a different approach to networking, one that might appear counter-intuitive. When networking, qualify every new connection and don't offer your card unless you are sure that this connection will fit into your Booked Solid Referral Marketing Plan[©], or that of your referral partners or sources.

The other qualifier that I would suggest is the infamous "gut" qualifier. If you feel comfortable with this person and enjoy their conversation, and they fit into the plan, by all means offer your card. If you are

125

not connecting well with them, you will be challenged to create the trust with them that will lead to a solid relationship with few problems and, most of all, the opportunity for a good referral. In that case, don't ask for their card.

It's a lot easier to motivate yourself to follow up if you have just a few people with whom to follow up and they are fellow networkers with whom you have really connected. So instead of trying to meet as many people as possible and acquire more cards than anyone else at the event, consider reformulating the goal of your networking efforts along the following lines: to meet at least 12 new people at a two-hour event, qualify heavily according to your plan, and exit with as few cards as possible, in anticipation of developing good relationships going forward.

4. Most networkers schedule their networking events without an eye to the time it takes to follow up.

Antidote: When you schedule your networking events, consider blocking in an extra 20-30 minutes of your time soon after the event and dedicate it to follow-up. Try to schedule the follow-up time as close to the event as possible. As mentioned in Antidote #2, stale-dating with your new connections happens much more quickly than you think.

5. Once these considerations have been reviewed and integrated into your mindset, you can find many technological solutions for implementing follow-up activities. LinkedIn is one prime example. It is a convenient and effective solution to the follow-up blues.

And there you have it, Antidotes to the "Follow-up" Referral Saboteur, and a process for vanquishing it and any others that plague you:

Drill down to the real story beneath the Referral Saboteur, learn referral marketing strategies to address the challenge and incorporate the solutions into The Booked Solid Referral Marketing Plan©.

Now you can bid a not-so-fond farewell to the "Follow-up" Referral Saboteur.

Thoughts to Review:

• Do I have a follow-up mindset that is fair to me?

• Do I unconsciously seek out business cards rather than good connections?

• Do I need a referral marketing plan for my new client development activities?

• Do I want to make sure that I reach my yearly business goals?

SABOTEUR #21 – THE "I REFUSE TO DEFINE MY IDEAL CLIENT" REFERRAL SABOTEUR

Statement #21: "I work with my ideal client." Never? Not often? Sometimes?

The "I Refuse to Define My Ideal Client" Referral Saboteur causes much damage to business professionals. It whispers persuasively into the ears of some that it is either too early, or too late, to identify the client with whom they want to do business.

Other business professionals who accept this Referral Saboteur come from a place of scarcity on this issue. They think that since they do not have any, or not enough, revenue coming in, they will take any business that comes their way.

Rather than defining their ideal client, they declare that they will do business with everyone and anyone. This Referral Saboteur reassures the business professional that it takes too much time to uncover the traits of their ideal client, that close enough is good enough.

The "I Refuse to Define My Ideal Client" Referral Saboteur nudges business professionals into resisting *the most important activity that they can pursue: to identify their ideal client.* In every way possible with a focus on avoiding missteps. As a review from Referral Saboteur #18, here is a short list of the characteristics that help define an ideal client:

1. Age and gender of the organization's leader

2. Role in the organization (Owner, V.P., Manager, Service)

3. Type of organization (Business, Government, Professional Service Provider)

4. Size of organization (Yearly Revenue, Number of Employees)

5. Behaviour style of leader (People like to deal with people who are like them)

6. Organizational values regarding the service provided

7. Personal values that the business professional is seeking in their ideal client

8. Level of motivation of the buyer

9. Budget commitment level

10. Problem that the client is experiencing that is addressed by the service

All of these characteristics are differentiators. They provide a clear picture to you and your network of the person with whom you would like to do business. The network member can take this picture, with all of its valuable differentiators, and share it with influential members of their own network. And thereby create referrals for you, the valued business professional.

The picture of your ideal client is especially motivating to the network member if it is accompanied by a moving success story. The right success story may take only a few seconds to share. I heard an excellent example of a short success story today delivered by a financial services expert: "When I was leaving their office, I saw that the receptionist was crying. When I asked her if she was alright, she answered that she was crying because her job was now safe because of the help I had given her employer in finding more working capital. She was so relieved. 'You saved 156 jobs today, John,' she said, 'I think that you ought to know that.'"

Wow! Do you have a picture of the impact of that business professional's services on his client's world? And of the size and sophistication of the organization? Did you learn about the pain of the receptionist and her employer? And what would have happened if they did not use the business professional's services?

Be sure to provide the most important information about your ideal client to your network in order that they may help you. Identify your ideal client as precisely, and as clearly, as possible. Add colour to your description with a success story. And never, ever, let the "I Refuse to Define My Ideal Client" Referral Saboteur take up a home in your inner landscape.

Thoughts to Review:
- Do I need to define my ideal client?
- Do I need to define my ideal client more precisely?
- Do I have a success story about my business and client relationships at my fingertips?

SABOTEUR #22 – THE "I'M AN INTROVERT" REFERRAL SABOTEUR

Statement #22: "I have the personality for networking. Never? Not often? Sometimes?

This Referral Saboteur highlights the pathway by which a simple personality trait, being an introvert, is hyperbolized into a reason for not attending networking events and not developing networking or referral-building skills. Introverts represent more than 50 per cent of the world's population and networking is the most powerful method for creating new business. Does it make sense for introverts to deny themselves the opportunity to create the revenue that they deserve due to a perceived weakness of their personality make-up? A Referral Saboteur, indeed, is at play here.

A very common, and quite lethal, Referral Saboteur is lurking in the statement, "I am an introvert; therefore, I can't be effective at networking." This Referral Saboteur assumes that there is some type of magic or mystery to revenue generation. This thought pattern suggests that only business professionals with special powers and personalities can be "rainmakers" and find their ideal clients.

Unfortunately, "I'm an Introvert" is yet another very dangerous Referral Saboteur.

If there is a *secret sauce to networking,* referral-building and selling, it is no more mysterious than a recipe from a Julia Child cookbook. The ingredients, the method and the execution are there for all of us to put together in a way that produces a final result of which we can be proud.

It will take time, motivation and focus to develop all of these skills, as well as an untamed burst of creativity; however, that is the case with any endeavour worth pursuing. And, really, is anything more important than learning about creating revenue for your business or practice?

This ugly Referral Saboteur whispers in the ear of an introvert to say that they are not the type of person who seeks out a public forum or who likes to do presentations or even bring attention to themselves when there are a number of people gathered at a networking function.

This Referral Saboteur asks the question, "How could you possibly do well at revenue generation when you are not comfortable with these activities?"

Fortunately, this myth about introverts has no basis in reality. In fact, introverts have many advantages over their extrovert colleagues when it comes to networking, referral-building and the sales process. Here are the top three:

1. Introverts are natural-born listeners. Listening is the key ingredient in the secret sauce of networking, referral-building and selling success. The business professional who listens well builds the high-quality relationships that create high-quality referrals, which result in much easier deal closures.

2. Introverts are less likely to talk over the client. It is not in the nature of the introvert to talk too much at a networking event or sales visit. And talking too much is the most likely, and damaging, error that an inexperienced business professional will make. In Julia Child's terms, an introvert is not going to add too much salt to the secret sauce because they want to express themselves. It is not how they are wired.

3. Most introverts like to follow a process. They will follow the recipe and retain all of the elements of the referral-building process that build more and better referrals. They will also be inclined to closely follow the steps that are fundamental to a standard sales process. There is still room for bold new ideas, however they are most effective when harnessed to the bigger picture.

In summary, introverts are more disposed to listen, keep quiet and follow a process. These three behaviours are keys to success with their network and prospects.

When you have learned how to execute effectively on a networking and referral-building plan and follow a sales process, you are a natural winner. Welcome to the world of revenue generation, introverts! Are you willing to watch the "I'm an Introvert" Referral Saboteur melt away like the Wicked Witch of the West of *Wizard of Oz* fame?

Thoughts to Review:
• Do I harbour the "I'm an Introvert" Referral Saboteur?

• Do I assume that success in revenue generation is like a secret sauce to whom only a chosen few may have access?

• Do I need training and development to manage my new client development process successfully?

Conclusion to the Referral Saboteurs

The Referral Saboteurs embody many of the damaging suppositions that business professionals have about networking that prevent them from achieving the referrals they so badly need from their network. Referral Saboteurs essentially prevent business professionals from conducting the activities that will serve them and their businesses.

With #11, The " I Hate Networking" Referral Saboteur, the business professional assumes networking is something very different from what it truly is, creating new relationships. Both Referral Saboteur #12, "No One Will Give Me a Referral" and Referral Saboteur # 13, "I Can't Refer Other People," discourage the giving behaviour that creates referrals. Referral Saboteur #14, The "Networking Does not Work" Saboteur, assumes that networking does not work and develops a self-fulfilling prophecy.

Referral Saboteurs #15, "I'm Not Comfortable Walking into a Room Full of People I Don't Know" and #16, "I Don't Like Meeting New People" send unhelpful messages about approaching a roomful of networkers and they discourage the essential act of networking: meeting new people. Referral Saboteur #17, "I Don't Like Small Talk," whispers that small talk is a waste of time, when, in fact, it is better seen as an important building block to communication that generates positive feelings about one's brand. Referral Saboteurs #18, "I'm Afraid to Give a Bad Referral," and #19, "I'm Afraid to Receive a Bad Referral" create fear about giving and receiving bad referrals, suppressing the very activity that will help to generate revenue for the business professional.

Referral Saboteur #20, "I Am Not Organized to Follow Up_on Referrals or Networking Opportunities" creates worry about follow-up to the point of not attending a networking event—leaving the business professional with nothing on which to actually follow up. Referral Saboteur #21, "I Refuse to Define My Ideal Client," limits the most important strategic move that a business professional can make: identifying their ideal client.

Finally, Referral Saboteur #22, "I Am an Introvert," concludes the Referral Saboteur section with a special bonus for anyone who has been giving a home to negative thoughts about networking because they see themselves as introverts and not as naturally outgoing as some of their colleagues.

Phil, Francesca and Joe: What Are Their Referral Saboteurs?

Phil, the Beleaguered Business Owner of 20 Years (X marks the Saboteurs affecting Phil)

> X Referral Saboteur # 11 The "I Hate Networking" Referral Saboteur
> X Referral Saboteur # 12 The "No One Is Going to Refer Me" Referral Saboteur
> X Referral Saboteur # 13 The "I Can't Refer Other People" Referral Saboteur
> X Referral Saboteur # 14 The "Networking Does Not Work" Referral Saboteur
> X Referral Saboteur # 15 The "I'm Not Comfortable Walking into a Room Full of People I Don't Know" Referral Saboteur
> X Referral Saboteur # 16 The "I Don't Like Meeting New People" Referral Saboteur
> X Referral Saboteur # 17 The "I Don't Like Small Talk" Referral Saboteur
> X Referral Saboteur # 18 The "I Am Afraid to Give a Bad Referral" Referral Saboteur
> X Referral Saboteur # 19 The "I Am Afraid to Receive a Bad Referral" Referral Saboteur
> X Referral Saboteur # 20 The "I Am Not Organized to Follow Up on Referrals or Networking Opportunities" Referral Saboteur
> X Referral Saboteur # 21 The "I Refuse to Define My Ideal Client" Referral Saboteur
> X Referral Saboteur # 22 The "I Am an Introvert" Referral Saboteur

Remember Phil? Phil's Sales Saboteurs had definitely reached "takeover" level, tracking at 10 out of a possible 10

135

Sales Saboteurs. Unfortunately for Phil, he was not doing any better with the Referral Saboteurs. He was providing home and hearth to 11 out of 12 possible Referral Saboteurs. Effective networking and referral-building mindsets include an ability to reach out from both the head, to learn new skills, and from the heart, to engage fellow network members.

Phil's world had become packed with worries, negative thoughts and many, many Saboteurs. As a result, his network had become very tiny as he moved deeper and deeper into his own spiral of withdrawal, and he was near depression. He was in no condition to leave the "cave" in his mind and start networking cheerfully with others in a broader world.

Phil's lack of knowledge about networking and referral-building had held him back for the previous few decades. He did not have the opportunity to learn that networking was about building strong relationships that create strong referrals. He was, therefore, very vulnerable to all of the Referral Saboteurs, including Referral Saboteur #11, "I Hate Networking," Referral Saboteur #14, "Networking Does Not Work," and Referral Saboteur #15, "I'm Not Comfortable Walking into a Roomful of People I Don't Know."

Given this ignorance about the power of deep relationships and referral-building principals, Phil's inner landscape fashioned a home for Referral Saboteur #12, "No One is Going to Refer me," Referral Saboteur #13, "I Can't Refer Other People," as well as Referral Saboteurs #18, "I Am Afraid to Give a Bad Referral," and Referral Saboteur #19, "I Am Afraid to Receive a Bad Referral." Not being an introvert by nature, Phil was not open to one Saboteur, Referral Saboteur #22, "I Am an Introvert."

A referral starts with trust. Trust is created in a relationship and is then transferred to other members of the business professional's network, *only* when there is the appropriate knowledge of the business, and ideal client, of the person whose services or products are being referred.

Phil was not receiving referrals from his network because he was not building his social capital, nor was he ready to grow his network. Since he was reluctant to meet new people, (Referral Saboteur #16), and felt that he was not organized to follow up with his network members, in any case, (Referral Saboteur #20), Phil had no tools to add to the breadth and depth of his network. He had no idea how to effectively direct his networking efforts.

As he became more isolated, Phil withdrew socially and was not able to reach out, giving in to Referral Saboteur #17, "I Do Not Like Small Talk." And, like many business professionals, Phil did not take the time to identify the characteristics of his target market, submitting to Referral Saboteur #21, "I Refuse to Define My Ideal Client."

Although Phil had many challenges ahead of him, his biggest challenge lay within — between his ears. He had 21 Sales and Referral Saboteurs to address.

Francesca, The Corporate Refugee (X marks the applicable Saboteurs):

O Referral Saboteur # 11 The "I Hate Networking" Referral Saboteur

X Referral Saboteur # 12 The "No One Is Going to Refer Me" Referral Saboteur

X Referral Saboteur # 13 The "I Can't Refer Other People" Referral Saboteur

O Referral Saboteur # 14 The "Networking Does Not Work" Referral Saboteur

X Referral Saboteur # 15 The "I'm Not Comfortable Walking into a Room Full of People I Don't Know" Referral Saboteur

X Referral Saboteur # 16 The "I Don't Like Meeting New People" Referral Saboteur

X Referral Saboteur # 17 The "I Don't Like Small Talk" Referral Saboteur

X Referral Saboteur # 18 The "I Am Afraid to Give a Bad Referral" Referral Saboteur

X Referral Saboteur # 19 The "I Am Afraid to Receive a Bad Referral" Referral Saboteur

X Referral Saboteur # 20 The "I Am Not Organized (Electronically or Otherwise) to Follow Up on Referrals or Networking Opportunities" Referral Saboteur

X Referral Saboteur # 21 The "I Refuse to Define My Ideal Client" Referral Saboteur

X Referral Saboteur # 22 The "I Am an Introvert" Referral Saboteur

What about Francesca, who already has four out of 10 Sales Saboteurs? Relatively new to the role of independent business professional, Francesca had not had as much time as Phil had to bury herself in Sales and Referral Saboteurs. However, her inexperience with networking had already created many Referral Saboteurs, with the result that Francesca had 10 out of a possible 12 Referral Saboteurs.

Her Referral Saboteur report card starts with positive results. As a former executive of a professional services firm, Francesca knew that Referral Saboteurs #11, "I Hate Networking," and Referral Saboteur #14, "Networking Does Not Work," were not helpful to a new client development environment. At the same time, Francesca had defined herself as "not a people person," which meant that Referral Saboteur #15, "I'm Not Comfortable Walking into a Roomful of People I Don't Know," Referral Saboteur #16, "I Don't Like Meeting New People," and Referral Saboteur # 22, "I Am an Introvert," were occupants of Francesca's mind. Francesca did not have a lot of knowledge about the value of "small talk" since she self-identified as "not a people person," and she had made a place for Referral Saboteur #17, "I Don't Like Small Talk."

Also, while Francesca had an appreciation for the need for networking, she was not equipped with any strategies for creating referrals. She had a long way to go with learning to create business by referral and she had a lot of questions and doubts about this new business development method. At different points in our conversation, Francesca had indicated that she was vulnerable to accepting the following Referral Saboteurs: Referral Saboteur #12, "No One Is Going to Refer Me," Referral Saboteur #13, "I Can't Refer Other People," Referral Saboteur #18, "I'm Afraid of Giving a Bad Referral," and Referral Saboteur #19, "I'm Afraid of Receiving a Bad Referral."

Francesca was concerned about her follow-up system and was letting this worry get in her way with Referral Saboteur #20, "I Am Not Organized to Follow Up on Referrals or Networking Opportunities." Finally, Francesca was new to marketing, let alone referral marketing, and she did not see the point of defining her target market, succumbing to Referral Saboteur #21, "I Refuse to Define My Ideal Client." Since Francesca had given a home to nine out of the 12 possible Referral Saboteurs, 13 Saboteurs in total, there was a lot of work for her to do. First of all, she had to examine her assumptions about networking, referral-building and "not being a people person." After she had embraced creating referrals as part of her lifestyle,

Francesca would feel the joy of creating referrals for life. And she'd want to do new business development *every* day.

Joe, The Business Owner without Sleep

    O Referral Saboteur # 11 The "I Hate Networking" Referral Saboteur

    O Referral Saboteur # 12 The "No One is Going to Refer Me" Referral Saboteur

    O Referral Saboteur # 13 The "I Can't Refer Other People" Referral Saboteur

    O Referral Saboteur # 14 The "Networking Does Not Work" Referral Saboteur

    O Referral Saboteur # 15 The "I'm Not Comfortable Walking into a Room Full of People I Don't Know" Referral Saboteur

    O Referral Saboteur # 16 The "I Don't Like Meeting New People" Referral Saboteur

    O Referral Saboteur # 17 The "I Don't Like Small Talk" Referral Saboteur

    O Referral Saboteur # 18 The "I Am Afraid to Give a Bad Referral" Referral Saboteur

    O Referral Saboteur # 19 The "I Am Afraid to Receive a Bad Referral" Referral Saboteur

    O Referral Saboteur # 20 The "I Am Not Organized (Electronically or Otherwise) to Follow up on Referrals or Networking Opportunities" Referral Saboteur

    X Referral Saboteur # 21 The "I Refuse to Define My Ideal Client" Referral Saboteur

    O Referral Saboteur # 22 The "I Am an Introvert" Referral Saboteur

Joe was a bit of surprise to me. He did not have the same number of Referral Saboteurs as Francesca and Phil. In fact, Joe had a lot of immediate opportunities to build his network, if he could rid himself of a single Referral

Saboteur. Joe had a deep, rich network, brimming with social capital that he could develop and leverage to create high-quality referrals for himself. Joe could double or triple his current revenue without difficulty by learning to leverage his network.

He had not given a home to Referral Saboteur #11, "I Hate Networking," or to Referral Saboteur #14, "Networking Does Not Work. Joe was a strong believer in the power of networking; he had received several pieces of business from referrals and was eager to build on his experience. So Joe had turned his back on Referral Saboteur #12, "No One Is Going to Refer Me," and Referral Saboteur #13, "I Can't Refer Other People," as he knew otherwise from his own business.

Joe had bought into the law of reciprocity a long time ago. The law of reciprocity happens when a member of your network helps you, and you, in turn, do everything that you can to help them. Joe had given and received good quality referrals so Referral Saboteur #18, "I Am Afraid to Give a Bad Referral," and #19, "I Am Afraid to Receive a Bad Referral," had no place in Joe's world.

He had a lot of confidence in his ability to provide good referrals. He also did not let Referral Saboteur #21, "I Am Not Organized to Follow Up on Referrals or Networking Opportunities," get in his way. Referral Saboteur #22, "I Am an Introvert," did not have a place in Joe's personality make-up, either.

Joe did need help, however, with learning to leverage his network for referrals. He did not know that there were at least 160 powerful referral marketing strategies available to him. He was delighted to learn that executing on just 40 of the 160 strategies would help him enhance his business relationships and double his revenue in one year.

The one Referral Saboteur that Joe knew that he needed to address was Referral Saboteur #21, the "I Refuse to Define My Ideal Client" Saboteur.

Joe wanted to learn about defining his ideal client and sharing this picture with valued members of his network, by using strong, compelling and moving success stories about the impact of his services on his clients.

He knew that clarifying and fine-tuning his message so his potent network could see the value he provided would have a major impact on his revenue for the next year.

In order to create the right compelling message, Joe would need to participate in the networking and referral-building training and coaching programs, outlined in Chapter 10, The Saboteur Antidote and Prevention Programs.

At a Saboteur Prevention Program, Joe would learn about capitalizing on his network by selecting "The Big 10," the 10 key people who would really help him grow his business and develop strategies together to help one another and create ongoing referrals for each other's business. This was the best investment that Joe could make in developing his business!

The Referral Saboteurs and You

Your Saboteur Self-Assessment answers will guide you to the specific areas that challenge you with the Referral Saboteurs. Have you read about every Referral Saboteur that corresponds to a "1, 2 or 3" answer in your Saboteur Self-Assessment for Statements #11-22?

What if you become aware of a Referral Saboteur that is not serving you, and it is not going away, in spite of your many efforts to rid yourself of it?

Perhaps, it is time to get some help?

Referral Marketing is the primary method for business professionals to create revenue. It is a specialized method of new business development that has not been effectively taught until very recently.

Even though referrals represent the oldest method of developing new business, the "how to create referrals" piece has been a challenge to understand, let alone teach, for centuries.

Now that the curriculum development strategies required to address both cognitive (head) and affective (heart) needs of learners of referral marketing are better understood, there are training and coaching programs available to assist with creating The Booked Solid Referral Marketing Plan© that builds referrals for business professionals.

You will find more details on these programs in Chapter 10 at the end of the book. Rest assured that help is on the way!

First, Chapter 7, the Antidotes to the Saboteurs, will provide more direction on reviewing any program on networking or referral-building that you might be considering.

And to reiterate the recommendations from the Sales Saboteur conclusion, please do pursue sales training courses that will help you to build your own effective sales-closing process. And develop a written sales process tool that you can take to every sales call. Better still, you might want to consider training and coaching programs that address all three skill areas: networking, referral-building and sales process development.

Make new business development behaviours a daily habit and your life will never be the same again. Welcome to the realm of enjoyable new business development activities, free of the Sales and Referral Saboteurs!

Thoughts to Review

- Do I have Referral Saboteurs?
- How many? Which ones?
- Do I want to do anything about them?Do I want to have fun developing new clients with a network of special people who I really enjoy helping and supporting? Who provide me with a steady stream of ideal clients?
- Do I want to develop my own Booked Solid Referral Marketing Plan© to determine my own daily new business development routine?

Chapter 7:
The Antidotes to the Saboteurs

Antidote: "A medicine or other remedy for counteracting the effects of poison, disease."

"Living by Your Wits is Knowing Where the Wasps Are," The Shining, *Stephen King*

The young man sitting in front of Derek was almost in tears. After torturous consideration, he had recently broken up with his girlfriend. There were also some mitigating circumstances that had created a complicated situation for him. Why was Derek privy to all of this drama? He was his boss. His sales manager, to be precise. And the young man was one of his stars. Derek's company needed their stars. Henry was a key player and it was critical that he advance the company's interests in two key meetings coming up that week. Henry needed to be, Derek needed him to be, at his best for those meetings.

Derek had come to know Henry quite well and was fond of him. He wanted to do the best for him and, of course, for the company. He realized that the only way that he could really meet all of these objectives was to help Henry with his immediate stressor—the choice before him about next steps with his girlfriend. The decision about his girlfriend was pressing but so were his fears and negative thoughts, the Saboteurs, which were coming out loudly and clearly in their discussion about the upcoming meetings with a key client.

Henry was very concerned about his ability to handle the meetings as he was having panic attacks and was not

145

sure if he would be able to manage one, if it happened in the meeting. The Saboteurs were playing hard with Henry and it appeared that they were not giving him any wiggle room. It was a difficult situation and both Henry and Derek were putting their heads together to help Henry through the next couple of weeks.

Without knowing it, Derek started a "coaching conversation" with Henry about his situation with his girlfriend. By asking or "placing" questions into the conversation, Derek was helping Henry talk through his problem while reaching down deeply into his being, to his heart, to find out what he really wanted to do. Derek did not want to colour Henry's final decision with any of his values or opinions, he wanted to help him make up his own mind. And so Derek asked him questions that would help him talk through his conundrum.

"Henry," he said, "I can see that this situation is terribly stressful for you and I'm sure you want to do what's best for you and Angela."

"Yes," Henry replied, "I know that whatever I do today, I will have to live with for the rest of my life. And I don't want to get it wrong. I want to be able to live with myself, whatever I do."

"So, Henry, what do you think is the best for everyone?"

"I hadn't planned on these complications; at the same time, I want to like myself when this is resolved."

"OK, you know how you want to feel about yourself. That's good. What do you see as the best solution for you and Angela?"

Derek and Henry discussed the situation together reviewing all sides of the problem. By the time Henry left the office, he was able to organize the pieces of his solution and identify his feelings as he considered his options.

He had talked out his problem and identified his fears. He was on the path for the decision that was right for him.

And his Saboteurs around his upcoming meeting had been managed—for the time being. He was ready to face his business challenges as he sorted out his personal issues.

Derek learned a lot from Henry that day. The Henrys of my world, sales professionals who touched my life and career, taught me that there was only one place where success in new business development begins and ends. Between the ears. Where our thoughts reside.

I learned that any problem, any doubt or fear that my team members carried about with them could, and would, have an impact on their performance, both in their business and personal lives. I also came to understand, through my own experience of working with all of these fine people, that identifying their fears, discussing them and defining a strategy for addressing them made a huge difference to them. And, ultimately, to their performance.

They would walk into my office, pale, stressed and burdened, have a discussion about what was really bothering them, and leave looking better and sometimes refreshed and motivated. The transformation from our conversations always surprised me. The power of "talk therapy" cannot be underestimated in expunging the Saboteurs.

Creating Success

The biggest challenge to creating success in your business, by far, lies in conquering or managing the Saboteurs. Isolating, addressing and expunging *as many* negative thoughts as possible is the real key to your success.

Negative thoughts, or Saboteurs, as the coaching world and I call them, hold all of us back from the life we deserve. These self-doubts, second thoughts and undermining voices in our own heads are responsible for many of life's losses. As we discussed in Chapter 2, whether it is Olympic podiums, sports teams, companies, organizations, families or individuals, it is the quality of the thoughts between the ears of the participants that best determines successful outcomes.

We hear about this principle of the power of thoughts in many places now. PMA, the acronym for positive mental attitude, is an example of this approach. If we are positive, we will attract positive results and avoid the problems that could so easily derail our efforts. And it is true. From the many pundits who have brought us *The Secret*, or PMA, to my first moment with this concept when I studied Pirandello's play entitled ***Right You Are Who You Think You Are*** in university, we have learned that positive thinking is very powerful — and very effective.

Over the last several decades, an entire self-help industry has emerged to assist us with managing our thoughts. This important and fascinating field generates about $11 billion yearly in North America, creating entirely new approaches to management, leadership, coaching (in and out of the sports world) and many other areas of human activity in its wake. And we are fortunate, deeply fortunate, to have access to this positive-thinking philosophy and psychology.

The challenge is that positive thinking, for all its beauty and ready accessibility, cannot embed itself into anyone's thoughts if there is a lot of background noise. That noise is the unique mix of those potentially 40,000 - 50,000 negative thoughts in every individual. The inner squabbling by the Saboteurs becomes a cacophony of fear and doubt that can paralyze the thought-holder for life and litter their world with difficulties—if they do not address these thoughts or self-limiting beliefs.

The work of Susan Jeffers in her landmark book, *Feel the Fear . . . and Do it Anyway*, is very helpful to those who are crippled by their fears. Some of the strategies Susan has spearheaded include positive self-talk, centring and instructing yourself to "turn it over to my Subconscious Mind and the Universal Energy."

Self-limiting beliefs, negative thoughts that become "truths" to the individuals who are harbouring them, can embed themselves from the time we are unsuspecting children. These negative thoughts burrow into the unconscious mind, where they are held and fed until their owners come to believe them, even if they are entirely irrational. Intellectually, people may reject the concept that they have embraced emotionally, creating boatloads of internal confusion. Ah, the power of the lizard brain.

The bottom-up sequence shown below demonstrates how negative thoughts build from the original "hurt" or "UGH" to a fully formed self-limiting belief,

THOUGHTS — Fully Formed Self-belief, "It will never work"

TH U GHT — "It often does not work in this situation."

T UGH T — "Things are not working out for me, I am not important."

UGH—the original hurt, "I am not important" (the real private hell)

UGH thoughts could include such ugly mantras as, "I am not important," "I am unlovable," "I will never be successful" or "I mean nothing."

These thoughts form the base on which scar tissue is built, moving from a self-limiting belief which starts as, "I am not important," in a five-year-old's world, all the way to, "This business will go nowhere," in a 45-year-old's professional life.As Stephen King points out in *The Shining*, "Living by your wits is knowing where the wasps are." The most important wasps to identify are the Saboteurs, our negative thoughts. In this book, the wasps in new business development have been identified and given names and cages, Sales and Referral Saboteurs. Now it's time to learn to conquer, manage or vanquish them entirely.

By the way, Henry did brilliantly at his meetings and the company was catapulted to a new level with one of their key clients. And, oh yes, Henry and his girlfriend are now doing very well, 20 years later. Derek went to their wedding and recently met up with Henry and saw pictures of their two kids.

Winning with the Saboteurs

As my knowledge of training and coaching business professionals in referral marketing strategies developed over the years, I came to understand the role of the Saboteurs in preventing worthy business professionals from creating the revenue and the success that they deserved.

I also came to appreciate the power of education in the eradication and prevention of the Saboteurs. When business professionals are properly trained and coached in the three skill sets that they require to grow their business or practice by referral, the Saboteurs have no place in their lives. They cannot find a foothold in a business professional's subconscious mind as their revenue grows and they attract more and better-quality referrals. Creating relationships for the pocketbook and soul feels magnificent!

I realized if business professionals could manage their Saboteurs via coaching, training, ongoing reinforcement, they're going to be successful, as long as they maintain a routine that supports their networking and referral-building activities. I developed a seven-step program that always, always, starts with expunging the Saboteurs:

1. **Manage and Anticipate Your Negative Thoughts**: Isolate, address, expunge or manage all Saboteurs. Be prepared for negative thoughts, name and cage all Saboteurs; make sure that you are truly aligned with your business.

2. **Take Care of Yourself:** The Saboteurs cannot find a home in a healthy body. Make sure that you get the exercise and sleep that you need. It is an obvious, and extraordinary, new business development strategy for all business professionals. Dr. Laura Crawford's many other strategies, outlined in this chapter, include experiencing nature, taking breaks to breathe, bringing music and creativity into your life, maintaining healthy hormones and a healthy digestive system, taking energy nutrients, hiring a coach and seeing your medical practitioner, naturopath and/or alternative health expert.

3. **Commit to Being Educated about New Business Development**: Understand that the Saboteurs thrive in ignorance. Learn and embrace the three skill sets of new business development: Networking, Referral-Building and Sales Strategies. Stay in the zone of success with The Booked Solid Referral Marketing Plan© and ongoing reinforcement training.

151

4. Set Goals and Feel the Moment of Victory Often: Setting the right intentions is also key to your success. Create very specific goals and think about your success; be sure to feel that moment of victory. Olympic medalists put themselves on the podium hundreds of times in their mind before they begin a competition, feeling and visualizing those victory emotions repeatedly. Saboteurs cannot reside in a mind that is that focused.

5. Develop a System for New Business Development Activities, The Booked Solid Referral Marketing Plan©: The Saboteurs are also shut out when business professionals commit to a system of daily, weekly, monthly and yearly activities that really grow their referrals and business. Business professionals need to learn best networking and referral practices to keep themselves accountable.

6. Commit to Lifelong Learning and Ongoing Reinforcement in New Business Development: Since new business development is Job #1 for all business professionals, make sure that you are always supporting your mindset with ongoing training. A referral marketing plan will keep you on track, along with ongoing reinforcement training. *Never* leave new business development to chance.

7. Enjoy the Ride: Joyful business professionals attract the best kind of referrals. Business professionals who are having fun bring their ideal clients into their business naturally. Positive energy breeds positive results.

Once you manage the Sales and Referral Saboteurs that limit your new business development activities, you can prepare yourself for the training and coaching outlined in Chapter 10 that will provide you with the mindset, strategies and tools to grow your business effectively, and joyfully.

It has been my mission so far in this book to assist with Step #1 and Step #2 of The 7 Steps to Creating Revenue for your business or practice. Step #1, *Manage and Anticipate Your Thoughts,* includes the following process with the Saboteurs:

1) Isolate or name your Saboteurs with the Saboteur Self-Assessment Tool

2) Address your Saboteurs and put them into cages with the 22 Saboteur categories.

3) Manage or expunge the Saboteurs with antidotes including "talk therapy," coaching and exploring the techniques of experts in the "fear" world, such as those offered by Dr. Susan Jeffers in her *Feel the Fear and Do it Anyway* book.

4)

Once the Saboteurs are managed or expunged in Steps # 1 and 2, you can move onto Steps # 3 –7 which include training and coaching programs in the three required areas of new business development: networking, referral-building and the sales process. Chapter 10 will provide you with more details.

Dr. Laura Crawford has compiled a list of effective strategies for addressing Step #2 of creating revenue for your business, *Take Care of Yourself.* Dr. Laura starts with daily practices to support your health, identifying the rituals that protect you, in the same way that a daily networking and referral-building routine will also advance your revenue and drive out the Saboteurs.

Daily Practices: Dr. Laura's Antidotes to the Saboteurs

The most powerful therapies are often the simplest. Because of this we find that there is no challenge to them, and/or we do not set aside the proper amount of time for them. In the following section, Dr. Laura suggests that taking time to implement these practices will help to decrease your stress response and increase overall performance and wellbeing.

The Healing Power of Nature

Helping to improve your focus and ability to complete tasks is as simple as making sure to take breaks to go out in nature. Some may prefer to "chunk" this into blocks of time at the cottage but studies are showing that spending time in nature on a daily basis can actually boost focus and concentration. Researchers at the University of Michigan had people take a stroll through an arboretum and administered performance tests afterwards. They found that memory and attention improved by 20 per cent after the walk. Later, a different research study tested people who had spent 10 minutes looking at a nature photograph and found that their focus increased by 10 per cent. The increase in focus and concentration was attributed to something called involuntary attention, which is the ability to have an expanded focus rather than a singular one. When you are in nature you can see the forest through the trees. This expanded view can help you look at challenges with a more productive perspective.

Breathing Breaks

One of the easiest interventions to implement is deep breathing. If we perceive stress or danger, our breathing becomes rapid and shallow; however, when we are relaxed we breathe deeply and rhythmically. Regardless of how we are currently feeling, we can switch our body from a stress response to a relaxation response by focusing on, and overriding, our breathing.

One simple breathing exercise is to breathe in for two seconds, hold your breath for two seconds, and breathe out for four to six seconds. Hold again for two seconds before starting the exercise again. To help focus further, you may choose to count actively within your head, which not only ensures that you are doing this correctly, but also focuses your mind on something other than the task that is causing you stress.

Music and Creativity

You cannot solve a problem with the same logic that created the problem. Engaging the creative brain, the right brain can help expand your thought process to find innovative solutions to everyday challenges.

One very easy way to do this is by being conscious of the music that you listen to while you are at work. At the Institute of Heart Math they have found that your body will adjust to the tempo of the music that you listen to. This means that if you listen to classical or other soothing music, you will experience lower blood pressure and decreased stress hormone. The music choice can be based on your preference, but be sure to be conscious of what response it creates within your body.

Exercise: Psychology Follows Physiology

Sometimes the trade-off between time spent exercising versus time spent at work feels like it is not worth it. However, investing in exercise can lead to many gains outside of improving your physique. One of the benefits of an exercise regime is that you improve your muscles and posture. Studies show that people who adopt posture that represents strength feel more confident in their decisions regardless of how they felt prior to adopting that posture.

This helps them hit their business targets while improving their relationships with the people in their business community. This can be a sure-fire way to beat the Saboteurs. Posture affects mood, energy and thoughts.

In addition to the confidence boost, exercise has a number of positive neurological effects. It stimulates the production of happy hormones, such as serotonin and dopamine, and it increases memory. It has also been shown to improve business outcomes and sales goals. A study published by the Journal of Small Business Management found that people who participated in regular aerobic exercise demonstrated better sales performance than those who did not exercise. Powerful bodies lead to powerful neurons, which can support powerful careers.

Sleep

Sleep is imperative for rest, recovery, and healing of the body and mind, but when we are stressed it is often the first thing to suffer. Our thoughts will keep us up at night as we try to solve tomorrow's problems; however, by the time tomorrow comes around, our neurons are so tired that we are unable to view situations clearly.

Sleep deprivation can be dangerous for both your health and your business. Studies have shown that if you average four to five hours of sleep or less per night for several nights, you will be operating at the same level of function as if you had been awake for 24 hours straight. Within 10 days the mind responds as if you had been awake for 48 hours. In a study assessing the impact of sleep on healing, people who did not get enough sleep took 40 per cent longer to heal than those who had regular seven- to eight-hour sleep patterns.

People who have irregular or poor sleep patterns are more prone to depression and they have been shown to make riskier business decisions. Furthermore, if you do not get enough sleep, your body is forced to run on adrenaline and cortisol, which activates the fight-or-flight response and leads to burnout. Sleep hygiene is the practice of creating a regular bedtime routine so that your body can get accustomed to sleep cues. Your body has specific sleep-wake cycles and relies on signals and habits to regulate the production of hormones related to sleep. There are several things you can do to ensure that these hormones are released at proper intervals. First, as best you can, try to go to bed and awaken at the same time every day. This will alert your sleep-wake cycle to the parameters under which it is operating. Second, avoid using technology such as computers or smartphones one hour before bedtime. The radiation from the screens has been shown to alter brain wave patterns and can affect your brain's ability to relax. And the hum of electronic equipment can keep people awake long after it's time to rest. Finally, try to sleep in complete darkness or wear a sleep mask. If there is light in the room your body will suppress the production of melatonin, the main hormone related to sleep, which will make it difficult for you to initiate sleep.

If you find that you are consistently having difficulties sleeping, it is worth speaking to your health-care provider, whether they be allopathic or alternative, to help rectify the situation. Sleep is not optional.

The body is the container of our emotions. If we don't support our container, then we cannot contain our emotional thoughts; they take on a life of their own.

Healthy Hormones

When your body moves into the stress response, it immediately mobilizes 1,400 enzymatic processes and 30 neurotransmitters and hormones. Hormone rebalancing is essential to stabilize the body after prolonged stress.

There are three specific areas of the body that are affected by the stress response. Let's start with the adrenal glands, otherwise known as the stress glands. These stress glands sit on top of your kidneys and are responsible for the production of the stress hormones cortisol and epinephrine (adrenaline). They are also involved in the regulation of blood pressure. When an individual becomes stressed, the adrenal glands immediately respond. If this stress response becomes prolonged or erratic the glands become "fatigued" and do not regulate themselves well. This can affect energy, drive, motivation, focus, memory, and many other systems.

The adrenal glands have an intricate feedback system with the thyroid gland. The thyroid gland is found just above the base of your throat and is responsible for energy production and metabolism. The thyroid is known as the main control centre of the body and it affects many systems including skin, hair, nails, digestion, and the heart. If the thyroid gland is working too hard it is called hyperthyroidism and can lead to heart palpitations, excessive sweating, inability to focus, anxiety and weight loss. If it is not working hard enough, or if other hormonal imbalances affect the thyroid hormones' ability to activate, a person will experience fatigue, hair loss, weight gain, depression, difficulty thinking or poor memory, and many other symptoms.

Finally, the gonads (ovaries in women, testes in men) become affected during times of stress also. The gonads secrete sex hormones such as estrogen and progesterone in women, and testosterone in men. If these hormones are out of balance, both sex drive and mood can be affected. Excessive amounts of estrogen, in women, and testosterone, can lead to anxiety, irritability, or anger. Too much progesterone can often lead to symptoms akin to depression or low mood.

Hormone treatment is very individualized; however, by managing the stress response, getting adequate sleep, and supporting healthy digestion you will help to support healthy hormones.

Healthy Digestion

Many people do not give any thought to what their digestive system is doing, unless they notice that things are not going as smoothly as they used to. The gastrointestinal system (GI system) is our energy delivery system; it is where we absorb the nutrients relevant to stress support and blood sugar balance. Though its primary function is absorption it is also involved in the regulation of mood and immunity.

Serotonin is considered the "happy hormone" in the body. Medication for anxiety or depression, often targets the serotonin receptors in the brain. What many people don't realize is that the healthy bacteria in your gut, called probiotics, make up 95 per cent of your serotonin. An unhappy gut can lead to an unhappy life.

In an experiment involving bacteria in the intestine, anxious individuals in one group were supplemented with probiotics while the other group was given a placebo. The group that was given the probiotics had less anxiety than those in the other group.

In addition to its effects on mood, the GI system also makes up 70 per cent of the immune system. It is involved in regulation and mediation of inflammation, immune response, and the identification of intruders in the body. In a world where getting sick can cause financial loss, maintaining a healthy intestine is a top priority.

Food sensitivities are a common contributor to immune dysfunction within the body. Food sensitivities are not true allergies. Consuming a food to which you are sensitive will not induce an anaphylactic response (such as people with severe allergies to peanuts, for example, will experience), but instead it can lead to a wide array of inflammatory reactions. This may manifest as bloating, headaches, IBS, constipation, weight gain/difficult weight loss, joint pain, and many other symptoms. To identify food sensitivities, you can adopt an elimination diet or you can request a food sensitivity test from your naturopath.

While the intestine can be a complicated system, there are specific measures that can be taken to support healthy function. First, consuming a diet that is rich in healthy protein, fibre, and fat will help to stabilize blood sugar and ensure that your body is receiving enough nutrients to repair itself. Second, finding a probiotic that is balanced for you may help improve your mood as well as your bowels. Finally, identifying food sensitivities may be imperative in decreasing inflammation and improving wellbeing overall.

Energy Nutrients

There are very specific nutrients that relate to energy and concentration. Specifically, vitamin B12 is necessary for the function of the nervous system and should be consumed during the stress response. Once symptoms of vitamin B12 deficiency become present, they are irreversible so it is imperative to make sure that you have enough. Vitamin B12 is involved in many functions including nerve repair, thyroid hormone production, blood cell production, and others. During times of stress and as we age, we do not absorb B12 effectively. Because of this, some people find vitamin B12 injections to be more effective than the oral supplement. This can only be performed through your naturopath or medical doctor.

Another nutrient that is involved in energy and concentration is iron. Iron is a nutrient that is available in many different foods. Some individuals, however, such as people who are iron deficient or women who menstruate and subsequently lose iron every month, require a larger amount.

Symptoms of iron deficiency include fatigue, heart palpitations, and dizziness. Since your lizard brain responds to internal signs of danger, such as heart palpitations, an iron deficiency can cause an individual to feel anxious all of the time. This can further perpetuate certain Saboteurs associated with that physical sensation. If you feel that your Saboteurs have a life of their own, it may be beneficial to determine if you have an iron deficiency.

Iron is not something that should be taken without performing a blood test first. Iron can build up in the body, and excessive amounts can result in iron deposits in the liver, brain, and joint tissues. This can cause pain, confusion, memory loss, and an inability to focus.

The adrenal glands, thyroid gland, and many other processes in the body rely on iron and B12 in order to function properly. By addressing deficiencies in these nutrients you will find that you are better able to manage your body's reaction to the Saboteurs.

Stop the Saboteurs in Their Tracks: Hire a Coach

As a health-care professional is to your body, so a coach is to your mind and thoughts. Relying on professionals to help you take care of the whole person means you'll be healthier, happier, and more successful all around—in body, mind, business and soul.

And when you hire a coach, hire a business coach. Being in business for yourself can feel very isolating. When we become stressed our body releases a hormone called oxytocin. Oxytocin is the same hormone that is released when we make physical contact with somebody. The purpose of having oxytocin circulate through our body when we are stressed is to encourage us to reach out to someone, perhaps to gain support or insight. A business coach gives you access to a professional who will support you and direct you in constructive ways. They are trained to support your vision, your values, and the strategy that will help you succeed. A coach can get to the core of what

161

you need to do and help you to be accountable and follow through on your plans.

Business coaches also help to bring perspective and logic to difficult situations. In a way they are your wingmen, completely looking out for your best interests. I have met many people who were so frustrated with their business that they were ready to "pack it in." One woman I know was frustrated because she believed she wasn't doing well, and she decided that she was ready to quit. Luckily, she called her coach who brought honesty, compassion and some rationale to the table. It turned out that the woman was set to make $400,000 that year but she was so emotionally drained that she had felt she was doing much worse. Her coach brought logic back to the business, saving her from making a regrettable mistake.

We have Saboteurs in all areas of our lives; however, we spend most of our adult lives at work. Saboteurs that stem from and affect our business and work ultimately seep into our relationships, self-care practices, and wellbeing. By identifying them and reining in the Saboteurs, the entire person reaps the benefits.

A Note about Dr. Laura Crawford and her Colleagues, Naturopaths:

Naturopaths are trained to optimize health so that you can perform to your full potential. Your naturopath can create an effective, targeted plan to produce specific results and eliminate problems in the maintenance of good health. They are trained in a variety of modalities including clinical nutrition, acupuncture, lifestyle counselling, mind-body awareness, and stress reduction.

When you have experienced ongoing stress, for example with the constant presence of the Saboteurs, naturopathic doctors can help you design a solution that will encompass many of the strategies that Dr. Laura Crawford has put forward in this chapter.

Your relationship with your naturopathic doctor should be a part of your relationship with your medical doctor. Be sure to let both of your doctors know about the interventions that have been prescribed to you.

Thoughts to Review:
- Do I get enough sleep?
- Does my diet support the energy output that I must sustain to grow and manage my business?
- Do I have any food sensitivities that may be masked by other symptoms like bloating, mood swings or afternoon fatigue?
- Do I feel really well? With lots of energy?

Conclusion to the Antidotes to the Saboteurs

Dr. Laura Crawford has provided you with many strategies for putting your body first, offering a valuable addition to the first step in the process, addressing your Saboteurs so you can take care of yourself. This helps you to be physically strong in order that you may implement the real antidote to the Saboteurs: managing your thoughts.

The best way for business professionals to manage their negative thoughts is to recognize that the brain is pre-disposed to support them. This predisposition is especially obvious when business professionals are going through major changes, which certainly include starting a new business or making a major transition from a structured corporate environment to your own business environment. It also includes the task of becoming your own brand. These are times when your unprocessed insecurities can have their way with your unsuspecting wellbeing.

So when you create your own revenue the best defence against the Saboteurs is to expect them. They are a natural part of the human condition and a natural part of creating a business. Expect the Saboteurs and then conquer or manage them.

Use the Saboteur Self-Assessment (SSA) tool and identify the origins of your negative thoughts. Do your negative thoughts arise from a lack of knowledge of how to create revenue and grow a business?

Or, do they come from ignorance about how to build new business? Do they stem from a lack of respect for the entire sales profession? Are they Sales Saboteurs? Or do your negative thoughts stem from an ignorance about appropriate networking, referral-building and sales closing activities? Or a lack of knowledge about managing networking conversations and strategic referral relationships? Are they Referral Saboteurs? Or, more likely, are your negative thoughts a combination of both Sales and Referral Saboteurs?

So, let's assume that the Saboteurs are defined. That they *are* named and caged.

Now what? Turn to the next Chapter to find out!

Thoughts to Review

- Do I manage my negative thoughts about growing my business? Have I identified those thoughts and their origins?
- Do I have the appropriate cages (strategies) for containing the Saboteurs?
- Do I know what my next steps are for both Sales and Referral Saboteurs?

Chapter 8:
Saboteur Prevention

"Treatment without prevention is simply unsustainable"
— Bill Gates

"You can't take the elevator; you will have to take the stairs."
- *A Booked Solid graduate.*

I was so excited about Saturday night. And not for me. For Francesca. She was receiving a business development award for extraordinary sales results. I could hardly contain myself. And, yet, I could not tell her about it. You see, her licencing organization had asked me to give her the award. She did not know that I was going to the ceremony and she didn't have a clue that she would be the recipient of the award. It was going to be a lovely surprise for her. And so well-deserved.

Francesca had worked very hard for two full years. She had exceeded all of her financial goals, and was earning a lot of money. And now she was going to be acknowledged by her peers for extraordinary performance in an area of competency of which she had known nothing two years earlier. Sometimes it is just too wonderful to do what I do, I thought to myself. Witnessing this minor miracle in Francesca's life had been keeping a smile on my face for the entire week.

So how did Francesca do it? She had not had any sales experience; she had been an engineer all her life. She had no compass in new business development. To quote the inevitable vernacular, "she could not spell 'new business development'" before she started learning about the three skill sets: networking, referral-building and the sales process. And didn't we establish that she had a lot of Saboteurs? In fact, she had a total of 17 Saboteurs: six Sales Saboteurs and 11 Referral Saboteurs. Fortunately, Francesca had many assets that supported her in her revenue creation journey. And, especially, with her battle with the Saboteurs.

Francesca's biggest asset? She was a lifelong learner. She believed in the power of learning. She believed that she would grow her business by growing her revenue creation skills, her networking, referral-building and sales closing skills. Her desire to win, as I have seen with other successful business professionals like her, is not about competing with her colleagues at their game. It is about doing whatever it takes, with a standard of impeccable excellence. This standard is supported by a high level of resilience and hearty self-esteem.

And Francesca sought out the help that she needed to succeed. Throughout The Booked Solid Referral Marketing Training Program© with her peers and during her one-on-one coaching sessions with me, Francesca pursued every detail that would improve her networking, referral-building and sales performance. No stone was left unturned, no new business tactic unexamined.

It did not matter if it meant many hours of networking on a weekly basis, endless coffees with members of her network or investing in an event for her network members that stretched her budget, Francesca always did what needed to be done to create her own revenue.

Happily, Francesca's love of learning and will to win were matched by the quality of the program and coaching that she had chosen to follow to grow her business. Francesca had needed a lot of help, and the right help with the right approach was there when she reached out for it.

Before we have a look at the program that helped Francesca so much, it is important to remind you that the antidotes identified in Chapter 7 can help a lot with reversing the adverse effects of the poison of the Saboteurs. In fact, they can bring you to your own ground zero and out of the Saboteur pit of despair. The antidotes on their own, however, will not, assist with helping you to move yourself forward powerfully with your new business development attitudes, behaviours and techniques. And certainly not to the level of achievement that was ultimately recognized by the people in Francesca's professional organization. Only the right training and coaching can do that for you.

Let's review the Seven Steps to Creating Revenue for Business Professionals:

1. Isolate, address, manage or expunge all Saboteurs.
2. Take good care of yourself.
3. Set the correct intentions (goal setting) and feel the emotions of victory.
4. Embrace lifelong learning about new business development as the primary strategy for protecting your revenue.
5. Learn about the attitudes and skills that lead to success, including networking, referral-building and sales-closing strategies.
6. Develop a system for your new business development activities that includes daily, weekly, monthly, quarterly and yearly plans. Commit to ongoing reinforcement through training and

coaching until you wind down your business and no longer require the revenue. Be open to change.

7. Oh yes, and enjoy the ride. Create a routine of new business development activities that you can embrace, working with people that you like, and who appreciate you as you like and appreciate them. Leave room for unexpected opportunities. The Booked Solid Referral Marketing Plan© helps you play more and work less, while growing your revenue joyfully.

Steps #3-7, setting goals, learning about the mind- and skill sets needed to grow your business by referral, developing a system and enjoying the ride are reviewed in the following selected "Saboteur Prevention Strategies." These tips provide an outline of the many pieces required to solve the revenue-success puzzle while keeping the Saboteurs out of the picture . . .

Saboteur Prevention Strategy #1:
Develop an Accountability MindSet with Your Networking and Referral-Building Activities

Twenty-two Saboteurs that prey on the new business development energy of business professionals have been clearly identified in this book. These Saboteurs sap your confidence and conviction. They are the "newts and salamanders" that reside within your unconscious mind and emerge when least expected, paralyzing your business and affecting your well-being. When your business does not grow, it can have a real impact on your family and lifestyle. With the Saboteurs, the best solution is prevention. In other words, just don't let them in.

168

The importance of an accountability mindset for new business development and its ability to conquer the Saboteurs cannot be overstated. If you are able to develop a creative daily plan of strategic and effective new business development activities, and are able to execute daily on those activities, you will literally send the Saboteurs packing. This is hard-won knowledge for a lot of experienced business professionals, including myself. The devil, of course, is in the details:

- What plan?
- What strategic and effective activities?
- How do I make sure that I do them daily?
- How will I find the time?

And, ultimately, where do I find the mindset to execute on a referral marketing plan that requires daily execution?

These fundamental questions underline the fact that creating revenue is not nearly as easy or as simple as many people assume. Remember the Sales Saboteurs? "Anyone can sell"? Sure—until you try it. And it is no easy or simple task to develop the plan outline for daily new business development activities.

- It takes time
- It takes focus
- It takes learning
- It takes knowledge
- It takes accountability
- It takes a new business development mindset

Since more than 90 per cent of business professionals generate their new business by referral, I suggest that the plan you develop is specifically designed to create referrals for your business or practice—a referral marketing plan that creates ongoing and high-quality referrals—forever.

The planning process includes understanding and articulating why you have embraced your chosen field and it sets out your vision, establishes your mission, makes meaningful goals and creates strategies, all of which is supported by an action plan. You need to review your action plans regularly, with the help of your coach, to ensure that you are always on track. Saboteurs, run for cover!

Let's finish with The Success Equation:

Your Referral Marketing Plan + Accountability = Prevention of Saboteurs + Solid Growth

Thoughts to Review:
- Do I have a healthy mindset for new business development?
- Do I have a plan for leveraging my relationships for new business?
- Am I willing to invest in creating a referral marketing plan for my daily activities?

Saboteur Prevention Strategy #2:
Create a Referral Marketing Plan
It's time to create your Referral Marketing Plan, one that is dedicated to leveraging the social capital that you have created, or will create, from your network.

As mentioned earlier, statistics show that referrals are the most common source of new revenue for business professionals. Dr. Ivan Misner, Hazel Walker and Frank De

Raffele polled 12,000 business professionals in a study that formed the backbone of their book ***Business Networking and Sex: Not What You Think***. Almost 90 per cent of survey respondents replied "yes" to the question, "Has networking played a role in your success?"

Let us not forget that average referrals, where some trust is transferred, enjoy a 34 per cent closing rate. Referrals are more readily closed than any other new business development method.

Imagine the closing rate of a referral that is truly supported by your referral source, someone who has listened well, knows all about the needs that your services address and sees clearly the solutions that you provide. And then imagine how it would feel if that referral source created an appointment for you, with the prospect, and even became a referral partner who would come to an appointment with a prospect, with you, and help you close the deal?

The result would be a closing rate as high as 80 per cent. Those are the results that you can expect from a referral marketing plan.

A referral marketing plan is developed by selecting and harnessing just 40 of the more than 160 referral marketing strategies available to you. More on them in Chapter 10. And you are empowered by your referral marketing plan to create referrals on an ongoing basis—for life. A referral marketing plan is all about *creating relationships for both the pocketbook and soul* with the kinds of people with whom you could build a referral relationship; they become your team of 8-10 key referral sources or referral partners.

What happens to the Saboteurs in the presence of a powerful referral marketing plan that is supported by training and coaching? They go away. Quickly.

Components of Booked Solid Referral Marketing Plan©

When business professionals select and develop 8-10 solid and strategic relationships with referral partners, and grow them with referral marketing principles, they can not only create business relationships for the pocketbook and soul, they will also enjoy referrals for life. So, to be specific, a referral marketing plan is created to provide the business professional with a road map for developing:

- the right relationships
- with the right clients
- with the right message
- with the right mindset
- with the right strategies and tools

All of which will build the right revenue and lifestyle for you. And being specific is key to creating a plan that will really work well for you, the author of the plan, with as few problems as possible. As the components of the Booked Solid Referral Marketing Plan© are unfurled below, you will note that specific direction in the following areas is very powerful, indeed, to any business professional:

Section #1—Self-Management
Section #2—Your Message
Section #3—Your Target Market
Section #4—Your Mission Statement
Section #5—Your Unique Selling Proposition
Section #6—Your Competitors
Section #7—Your Infomercials
Section #8—Your Contact Sphere
Section #9—Your Network Choices

Section #10—Your Relationships
Section #11—Your Asks
Section #12—Your Referral Sources and Partners
Section #13—Your Tactics to Grow Relationships
Section#14—Form Referral Partnership Relationships
Section#15—Your Campaign Plan
Section #16—Your Budget
Section#17—Reward Referral Sources and Partners
Section #18—Your Sales and Referral Projections
Section # 19—Your Tracking and Evaluation Tools
Section # 20—Your Benchmarks and Celebrations

By creating a plan and participating in networking and referral-building programs, more details for which you will find in Chapter 10, you can create the revenue that you truly deserve.

Saboteur Prevention Strategy #3:
Enjoy the Journey: Skill Sets Needed to Become a Successful and Joyful New Business Developer

Many professional service providers are surprised to learn that the new business development process is far more complex than they may have thought. After all, what can be so difficult about finding a prospect, selling them on your services and converting them to client status? You know what you do, why wouldn't they buy?

Professional service providers who have tried, with or without success, understand that building new business is no easy task. As you may have experienced, doing poorly with revenue growth can even take the joy out of everything that you do. And provide fertile ground in which the Saboteurs can flourish.

Let's summarize: there are a total of three skill sets corresponding to the three stages of business success that lead to joyful new business development. Those skill sets must be supported by a plan, and you must be accountable to the plan, until the day that you close or sell your business. Do continuously increasing levels of success appeal to you?

3 Stages = 3 Mindsets = 3 Skill Sets

They correspond to:
1.   The Introduction: Networking Skills
2.   Business Development: Relationship-Building Skills
3.   Closing for Business: Sales-Process Skills

Stage One ~ The Introduction: Networking Skills:

The ideal way to create a new client is through a referral. Referrals, defined as a transfer of trust, have a much higher closing rate and they are often less sensitive to price. By networking thoughtfully and effectively, you can select members of your network who will want to generate business through powerful referrals, like you do. Learn networking skills to create and select relationships that will generate referrals for you. You will be surprised to discover that 8-10 relationships will deliver dramatic results! In this stage, remember to be aware of the Sales and Referral Saboteurs we identified earlier in this book. They are more than ready to undermine your networking efforts, if they are not conquered or managed.

Stage Two ~ Development: Relationship-Building Skills:

Strong relationships form strong referrals. A strong relationship in the referral world is one where your referral source likes and trusts you, and understands your business

174

very well. Armed with this business overview, a giving nature and dedication to the details, your referral source can do wonders for your business. Your job is to learn as much as you can about your referral partner's business as well— their customer needs and the solutions they provide. Your referral source must learn the same information about you. If your referral source and you share the same target market, you might be referral partners and can create referrals for life. Isn't it interesting to know that there are more than 18 tactics to move the right relationship forward to this type of referral success? Again, watch out for those Sales and Referral Saboteurs.

Stage Three ~ Closing for Business: Sales-Process Skills:

You can be the keeper of excellent networking skills, be a superb relationship builder and fail to close business when a referral is given to you. If this describes your situation, you may find that you need help with a sales process. This stage of new business development requires a very different mindset from Stage One and Stage Two. Working with an expert, you can develop your seven-step sales process, paving the way for a written sales process. You can then enjoy closing sales, with complete authenticity. Knowing how to manage meetings with your prospects is critical to your success at this stage, as is watching for the Sales Saboteurs. Create the sales process with your coach and develop a strong plan in order to defeat them at their own game.

Stage One of creating new clients by referral requires a nurturing yet qualifying posture to select the right relationships for generating referrals. Stage Two involves business relationship-building skills to move the relationship towards referral creation mode. Stage Three represents an entirely different mindset, which is driven by short term results, closing the business and locking in the revenue. These three stages represent three different mindsets, and three different skill sets.These skills are not learned overnight. It takes at least a year to learn and master all three of these skill sets, and at least another year to build a powerful network to support the long-term growth of your business. Two years in total for the development of a top notch network. And the ongoing accountability to your daily, weekly and monthly new business development activities never stops. Please see Chapter 10 for an overview of Booked Solid programs for creating the revenue that you deserve, and the plans to get you there. Remember the graph that I showed Phil, who was definitely not feeling joyful about new business development when we spoke for the first time? It will remind you of how all of these components fit together, enabling you to reap the fruits of your own networking, referral-building, and sales-closing efforts:

Networking	Referral Building	Sales Strategies
F A R M E R	G A R D E N E R	H A R V E S T E R

PLAN & ACCOUNTABILITY

Thoughts to Review:

•Do I have all three of these skill sets? If not, which skill set(s) am I lacking?

•Do I have a plan for creating referrals for my practice or business?

•How much joy will I feel when I've complete control over my new business development?

Rome Wasn't Built in a Day . . . Building Your Business Takes Time and Perseverance

So, it takes a year to learn the three skills of new business development. At least. And another year to execute on your learning and to develop the network that will truly serve your business growth.

So, two years, in total, to build your skills and become an expert referral marketer with a solid network built for the long term. Maybe even for the rest of your business life, if you want to make sure that you are always committed to excellence in the networking, referral-building and sales strategies that will build your revenue.

Francesca, for example, is never going to abandon her training and coaching program. She has too much riding on it; she knows that her business will suffer if she does not continue to grow her new business building skills and create new social capital every day by following her Booked Solid Referral Marketing Plan©.

As highlighted in the tips above, at least a year of training and coaching is needed for the development of all of the key new business development skills that are required to create extraordinary results. This training and coaching program must also be coupled with a rigorous program of focused, daily referral-building activities. Since the Saboteurs are wily and subversive, and their challenges can be complex, the construction of the remedies and solutions needs to be all-encompassing. And continuous.

A second year of training, coaching and reinforcement training is required as you grow your network and move through and complete the four phases of a high quality network.

To quote sales guru David Mattson, "Do the behaviors, do the behaviors, do the behaviors." The primary action to creating new business development success is to embrace the fact that the right activities must be done every single day. With a close eye on the details that make a difference to the bottom line. Daily new business development activity was the first key to Francesca's success, and it was one of her main antidotes to the Saboteurs.

By engaging and moving herself forward every day toward her goals with The Booked Solid Referral Marketing Plan©, Francesca was able to build her social capital with her current and new network members.

With her current network members, Francesca was able to save a lot of time by leveraging all of the trust that she had built over the years. She was able to create a referral team from selected members of her network, teaching them about her new business and asking them to help her with introductions to her ideal client.

And did I mention that Francesca was *my* ideal client? A motivated business professional with a specific expertise, who is a lifelong learner and a giver, committed to her own professional development and ready to do what it takes to grow her revenue. Being specific about your ideal client is one of the cornerstones to referral marketing success.

Francesca knew exactly the characteristics of *her* ideal client and was ready to share those qualities with her network. Members of her network came forward with the introductions that Francesca needed to grow her business and create extraordinary results.

Francesca had become strategic with her network members while remaining respectful. She approached members of her network with a request for help, not for business.

Please note that Francesca did not take a direct selling approach with her network. She was very clear about the help that she needed; however, at the same time, she was not promoting herself inappropriately, not "selling," to members of her network.

Conclusion to Chapter 8 – Prevention

Francesca came to appreciate that new business development involved a lot more than she ever thought it would. She looked at the entire sales world differently and she shopped differently, always maintaining respect for the challenging role of salespeople. She bought differently, looking for the value/price equation, instead of only price.

Francesca had learned there was a direct relationship between the way she purchased products and services and the way that she sold her services to her clients. She had learned that as you purchase, so do you sell.

Most importantly, Francesca had adopted a proactive mindset about business development. She had embraced the positive attitude that the right daily new business development activities would grow her business by high-quality referrals.

Her actions were grounded in The Booked Solid Referral Marketing Plan©. She was supported by ongoing reinforcement and accountability with training and coaching.

Francesca came to enjoy creating her business by referral, surrounded by like-minded members of her network who supported her and believed in her. Just as she believed in them.

Together, they had created relationships for their pocketbook and soul. They were in control of the future of their businesses, and their results made them proud. Francesca was finally creating the revenue that she deserved.

And the Saboteurs? What Saboteurs?

Chapter 9:
Oh the Places You'll Go

Oh, the places you'll go! There is fun to be done!
There are points to be scored. There are games to be won.
—Dr. Seuss

I was smiling to myself. I had just heard from Joe. He was calling to tell me how well he was doing. We had done a lot of coaching together over the year. As a result, he had been able to wrestle his Saboteurs to the ground.

He had come to recognize that his so-called "business issues" were not about business at all. Joe had worked out that he needed to re-frame his relationship with his family. And, as a result, he was able to re-design his relationship with his spouse.

His partner in life was delighted to have the man with whom she had fallen in love back with her again.

And Joe was delighted not to be held back by the Saboteurs any longer. Since the re-framing and re-designing of his relationships, Joe was able to implement a plan of the right daily activities that really grew referrals and his business. And to enjoy creating the right referral relationships for both his pocketbook and his soul.

He was calling me to invite me to dinner to celebrate his success with him and his spouse. He had landed the one account that would really change his life. Sometimes it is too wonderful to do what I do.

New Business Development Joys: Developing a Lust for Opportunities

The flip side to the new business development blues are the highs that you can experience when you are on the hunt for a new business opportunity.

Creating new business for your business is a joyful and fun experience. Embrace these moments of victory. Remember them. And, most importantly, seek them out!

If you are emotionally connected to experiences in a positive manner, you will seek to revisit those moments. Keeping this pleasurable thought about new business development, and filing it into your DNA will help your new business growth immeasurably.

When I witnessed some top new business development experts plan for a new piece of business this week, I could feel their love for the possibilities, their joy and, ultimately, their love for the hunt!

There is a focus, even a type of sales lust, for those who are used to winning at the big-game hunt of closing on new business.

Developing this posture of confidence, this winning mindset around new business, is one of the most important strategies for business success.

And Then, There's Phil. Remember Phil?

Let's go back to that day, that awful day that Phil and I met in the coffee shop, and pick up from there.

Phil and I discussed the fact that he was holding onto some serious Saboteurs. In fact, Phil was loaded with

Saboteurs. To his credit, Phil had identified that he needed coaching to assist with his new business development challenges. It was an excellent place to start.

He wanted to be fixed, build up his client base and make enough money to delegate everything to do with new business development to a hired gun, a sales professional.

I had to break the news to Phil that fixing his situation was going to be a journey, an odyssey, in fact.

Also, Phil would be well advised to re-consider ever abdicating his role as a new client development force in his company, no matter how large or successful he became.

Phil's ideal approach was to make sure that looking after the details of new business development would be his #1 Job, every day, until the day he sold or closed his business.

I explained to Phil that when you are the brand, there is a lot to learn about creating your own revenue. Building the business of your dreams involves learning about *how* to create new business by referral.

Phil embraced his Booked Solid training and coaching program and was a most enthusiastic member of his classes.

No longer isolated, Phil became friendly and very approachable. Once he had created his referral marketing plan, he continued to be active in his local referral marketing community, creating high-quality referrals that always translated into ideal clients for his business. He was, and still is, a delight in the class and in one-on-one coaching sessions.

Phil's real issue? He had not been aligned with his 20-year-old business for many years; he no longer had a personal and vital passion for it.

When he redefined his business, however, Phil's world changed. He became truly aligned with his business purpose and he learned how to joyfully create his own revenue.

And the Saboteurs left Phil's life.

I was delighted to write the following Monday Morning Referral Tip to celebrate the growth I had witnessed in all of the business professionals with whom I had the privilege to work, including Phil, Francesca, and Joe:

The Perfect Networking Event

Last night I went to the perfect networking event in my referral partner's community. Here's what I noticed:

1. Networkers didn't move aggressively towards other networkers, ignoring open/closed body language; nobody pounced into conversations without permission.

2. People didn't hand out their business cards without a request from their fellow networker.

3. No business professionals breathlessly and shamelessly promoted their business.

4. Networkers didn't try to sell others on anything.

5. Nobody seemed worried about the size of the group.

And here's what else I noticed:

1. Everyone was trained in networking. They understood that networking is about opening relationships which, when strategically developed, will lead to high-quality referrals.

2. Everyone was listening intently to their fellow networkers, providing their colleagues with complete, focused attention in a caring and supportive manner.

3. Everyone had learned how they could help one another and they were connecting members of their network at every conversation.

4. Everyone was smiling at one another, moving about the group, greeting one another with heart-felt good wishes.

5. Everyone was introducing new members of their network, guiding them towards those members of their network who could and would want to help their new contact.

6. Everyone knew who they wanted to meet but were patient about first helping others make their desired connections.

7. Everyone won. More relationships were created and more referrals exchanged than in a group of twice or three times the size.

8. Most important of all, everyone understood that it was the quality of the people in the room, not the quantity, that mattered.

I was thrilled. I will let Dr. Seuss have the last word:

And will you succeed?
Yes! You will, indeed!
(98 and 3/4 percent guaranteed.)

KID, YOU'LL MOVE MOUNTAINS!

Chapter 10:
The Saboteur Antidote & Prevention Programs:

Want to Stop the Saboteurs?

•Invite Paula to energize and inspire your group by going to www.bookedsolid.ca/speaking or calling 905-383-0355.

•Explore Booked Solid Programs for ways your organization can move forward – go to www.bookedsolid.ca/onsite or call 905-483-0355

•Have a look at Booked Solid online programs – they have helped countless others just like you to succeed – go to www.bookedsolid.ca/homestudy

•Consider Coaching with Paula – go to www.booksolid.ca/coaching to explore your options and see whether working with Paula is right for you

•Sample the Monday Morning Referral Tips – go to www.bookedsolid.ca/referraltips

Do you create revenue for your organization or yourself?

Do you have Saboteurs that hurt your revenue and your brand?

Ready to do something about them?

The Booked Solid Programs for Saboteur Antidote and Saboteur Prevention are designed to help you get serious about your Saboteurs. *Now.* These programs have helped countless others free themselves from self-sabotage and create the revenue that they deserve.

Invite Paula to Speak at Your Organization's Main Event:

Please feel free to extend a personal invitation to me to speak at your next major event or conference. I will ensure that your organization embraces the real challenges faced by business professionals who create their own revenue. I am a professional and enthusiastic speaker with decades of experience and I can nail any topic found in either the Saboteur Antidote or Saboteur Prevention Programs. More than that, I realize that this is a challenging topic and I appreciate how negatively the Saboteurs can affect the bottom line of an organization of almost any size.

Want to know more? Let's talk, call Paula at 905-483-0355 to set up a time for a conversation or visit www.bookedsolid.ca/speaking.

Interested in Bringing Booked Solid Programs to Your Organization? Explore Booked Solid Programs to dramatically increase your new business. The Booked Solid Programs are focused on two major categories,

1) Saboteur Antidotes

2) Saboteur Prevention

These programs delve into great detail about how Saboteurs are developed, what they are, how to get rid of them and what is possible once they stop interfering with your organization's success. They are delivered, online and/or on-site, at your organization's training facilities. Watch for the jaw-dropping increase in revenue!

188

To learn more about Booked Solid Programs for organizations, please go to www.bookedsolid.ca/onsite or call 905-483-0355. We'd be delighted to speak with you.

Interested in Taking Booked Solid Programs for Creating The Revenue that You Deserve? Concerned about your Saboteurs? Ready to do something about them? At your own pace and convenience? Check out the Booked Solid Saboteur Antidote and Saboteur Prevention Online Programs designed to help you conquer your Saboteurs when the time is right. Create the revenue that you deserve. Free yourself of the Saboteurs. You'll never look back! To learn more about online Booked Solid Programs that are convenient for you, visit www.bookedsolid.ca/homestudy.

Coaching with Paula www.bookedsolid.ca/coaching. If you are dedicated to your own success and ready to move forward, you might be a great candidate for my one-on-one offer. If so, here's what you can expect:

1) A Partner in doubling or tripling your revenue

2) Your Booked Solid Referral Marketing Plan refreshed at all times

3) Accountability for all new business activities

4) A written 7 step sales process

5) A Pre-Call Planning and Post Call Debriefing relationship

If these outcomes resonate with you, please go to www.bookedsolid.ca/coaching and complete the online assessment.

Want some advice on the Saboteurs every Monday Morning? www.bookedsolid.ca/referraltips. The Monday Morning Referral Tips are there for you every week. If you would like thoughtful and in-depth advice on the Saboteurs *and* on new business development by referral, you might want to think about signing up for the Monday Morning Referral Tips. Stop the Saboteurs from coming back. And you can unsubscribe at any time. If you are interested, please go to www.bookedsolid.ca/referraltips.

Want to hear about my next book?
You'll be the first to know the details. Please go to www.bookedsolid.ca/referraltips.

Chapter 10 - Dr. Laura Crawford, ND

Dr. Laura offers comprehensive health programs tailored to the needs of the individual or the organization utilizing a multi-disciplinary approach. If you are interested in learning how you can protect yourself or your company from burnout or otherwise want to improve overall health and wellbeing, visit Dr. Laura at www.drlauracrawford.com.

Dr. Laura is an accomplished speaker who has spoken on a variety of topics including
- Brain Health

- Protecting Yourself from Stress

- Women's Health in the Workplace

- Nutritional Habits for Success.

To book Laura to for a speaking engagement, please visit her website at www.drlauracrawford.com/speaking.

About the Author

Paula Hope helps business professionals create the revenue they deserve.

She speaks, writes, trains and coaches business professionals to conquer their Saboteurs by growing their networking, referral-building and sales process skills. She is a leading expert on referral marketing and strategic networking, owning her own business, aptly named "Booked Solid".

With her 30-plus-year sales and marketing career, Paula developed her sales wisdom and compassion for those on the front lines of new business development.

With *Stop The Saboteurs*, her first book, Paula applies decades of expert experience to offer solutions towards conquering the self-destructive fears and self-limitations that can impede success. This breakthrough book provides invaluable advice previously only available to her many clients, for whom she has worked wonders in helping them overcome negative thoughts to turn failure into triumph.

Paula and her partner, David, live in The Blue Mountains on Georgian Bay. Together, they have four talented and beautiful daughters, four special grandsons and four wonderful dogs. When not petting their dogs, Vivid and Paris, Paula loves to travel, read and play tennis.

Manor House
905-648-2193